Tales from the Sak-Sak

Doing Nasho in New Guinea

Edited by

Max Quanchi

Quanchi Pacifika Publications

BRISBANE, QLD, AUSTRALIA

Copyright © 2021 by **Max Quanchi**

All rights reserved. No part of this publication may be reproduced, distributed or transmitted in any form or by any means without prior written permission.

Quanchi Pacifika Publications
Email: quanchi.amqfu@gmail.com

Publisher's Note: This is a work of non-fiction complied from actual events contributed by:

Laurie Bowman
Rick Larsen
Bob Mason
Max Quanchi
Peter Suna
John Sweeney

Illustrations, Maps, Appendices, Notes, Index, 257 pp

Tales from the Sak-Sak – Doing Nasho in New Guinea, edited by Max Quanchi. -- 1st ed.
ISBN
Paperback 978-0-6451576-0-4
Ebook 9780645157611

Tales from the Sak-Sak – Doing Nasho: In New Guinea

is jointly authored by:

Laurie Bowman
Rick Larsen
Bob Mason
Max Quanchi
Peter Suna
John Sweeney

Bob wrote several hundred hand-written pages to start off the writing process and then everyone chipped in their own stories and photographs. Max added stories he found in a hundred letters he had sent home to his parents, and then prepared the draft and edited the text for publication.

The final result, *Tales from the Sak-Sak, Doing Nasho: In New Guinea* was a joint-authored effort by six old blokes remembering their youth, Nasho and New Guinea

CONTENTS

ACRONYMS AND FOREIGN TERMS 5
PROLOGUE 7
SIX NASHO SERGEANTS 21
BASIC TRAINING SALUTING and MARCHING 41
CORPS TRAINING and then to PORT MORESBY 53
LIFE AT MOEM BARRACKS 67
MATTERS EDUCATIONAL 91
MATTERS MILITARY 103
ON PATROL 113
ORDERLY SERGEANT DUTY 131
VANIMO 137
DINING-IN NIGHTS, SMORGASBORD AND AMAZING FISH STEAKS 151
A SPORTING LIFE 163
WEWAK: GOING TO TOWN 175
SEARCHING FOR MISSING PLANES 183
RADIO BLONG YUMI 189
LITTLE RED RENAULT AND A NIGHT TO REMEMBER 193
LCSWTD 199
FISHING 203
ARMY VERSUS NAVY 209
GOING HOME: AFTER NASHO 215

FINAL COMMENT ON DOING NASHO in NEW GUINEA 235
APPENDICES 239
   A   CERTIFICATE OF DISCHARGE FOR BOB MASON, FEB 1968 241
   B   INTERIM CERTIFICATE OF DISCHARGE FOR BOB MASON, FEB 1968 243
   C   LETTER FROM ARMY DIRECTORATE OF EDUCATION, SEPT 1967 245
   D   LETTER FROM MINISTER OF VETERANS AFFAIRS, ND 247
   E   WHY IS AUSTRALIA INVOLVED IN VIETNAM? AACE CURRENT AFFAIRS HAND-OUT 1968 249
   F   MOEM AREA SPORTS NOTICES, 25 SEPT 1967, 2PIR MOEM BARRACKS (EDITED BY MAX) 251

GALLERY
Scenes from 1966 –67

View from Max's bedroom during Monsoon season, to reef opposite the Sgts Mess, 1966

Sergeants Mess "Haus Win", 1966

Max water skiing in front of Sgts Mess, Vanimo

Laurie, with Lt Kenneally and Lt Franklin offshore at Vanimo base, 1966

Off to Brandi beach for body-surfing – Laurie in the lead, Rick, John and Max to the right

New Married Quarters for ORs, taken from the water tower (Muschu Island in background), 1966

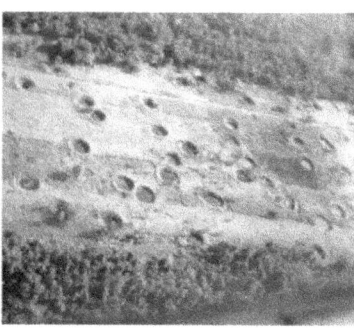
Bombed Japanese airstrip near Aitape in 1966

Meeting the locals on patrol near Telefomin, 1966

Wewak looking out to sea, taken from a Caribou coming in to land at Wewak

Caribou, the Army's aerial workhorse. Loading at Wewak for a patrol 1966

Four Army Medals awarded to the Nasho Six for service in TPNG 1966-67

Pick dressed up for 'Pacific Night' in the Sgts Mess.

Max in action with Pick in the Wewak v Madang AFL game 1967.

ACRONYMS AND FOREIGN TERMS

AFL	Australian Football League (known as "Aussie Rules")
Bilum	*Tok pisin* for Woven fibre (string) bag used for a multitude of carrying purposes
CB	Confined to Barracks (a form of punishment for wayward soldiers)
CO	Commanding Officer, at Company, Battalion and Regiment level
CSM	Company Sergeant Major, a senior NCO rank, one below RSM
DC-3	Douglas DC-3, USA-made, twin-propeller transport (often converted for passenger traffic after WWII)
Didiman	*Tok pisin* for Agricultural Extension Officer
Haus boi	*Tok pisin* for a 'house boy' or servant, often a mature aged man
Haus win	*Tok pisin* for a local material building with open sides to let the breeze blow through
HMAS	Her Majesty's Australian Ship
IACE	Intermediate Army Certificate of Education
IOE	Intermediate Oral English certificate
Kiap	*Tok pisin* for Australian administration patrol officer
Koteka	*Tok pisin* for Penis gourd
Lakatoi	*Tok pisin* for a large double-hulled canoe with a single lateen sail (but usually powered in the 1960s by an outboard motor) (a Motu word from Papua originally)
Lap lap	*Tok pisin* for term for wrap-around, imported material clothing (like a sarong)
LBW	Leg before wicket (cricket term)
LEP	Locally Enlisted Personnel
LSM	Navy acronym for a front-end loading, Landing Ship Medium
MAL	Mandated Airlines (officially Ansett-MAL)

NCO	Non-Commissioned Officer (Sergeant, Sgt-Major, Warrant Officer, CSM and RSM)
OR	Other Ranks (privates, below the rank of NCOs)
PCOE	Proficiency Certificate in Oral English
PIR	Pacific Islands Regiment
2PIR	2nd Battalion, Pacific Islands Regiment
PNG	Papua New Guinea (name taken on independence in 1975)
PNGVR	Papua New Guinea Volunteer Reserve
RSM	Regimental Sergeant Major, the top ranked NCO
SACE	Senior Army Certificate of Education
Sak-sak	*Tok pisin* for local building materials (thatch leaf, bamboo, and timber)
STOL	Short Take Off and Landing (aircraft)
Swan	Army slang for a free trip, supposedly taken as a duty
Tok Pisin	*Tok pisin* English, slang, and the lingua franca language
TPNG	Territory of Papua New Guinea; The Australian Territory of Papua combined with the Trusteeship of the United Nations (New Guinea)
Wantok	*Tok pisin* for 'one-talk', or friend, clan or family speaking the same language
WO	Warrant Officer (Class I, or Class II)

CHAPTER ONE

PROLOGUE

These stories about six young men sent in 1966-1967 to the Territory of Papua New Guinea (TPNG), an Australian colonial possession, are also stories about the compulsory military conscription program known in Australia as National Service which ran from 1965 to 1973. Historians have focused on the conscription debates over compulsory military service, by ballot, for twenty-year-olds in Australia, the Vietnam War and the anti-war Moratorium demonstrations, so we thought it was time to add a personal perspective of Nasho, not of serving in Vietnam or for two years in bases around Australia, but of spending two years in uniform, living and growing up on the island of New Guinea in the 1960s.

By offering these vignettes, tall tales and actual events, we hope to present the other side of National Service or conscription, not as a national, political controversy over what turned out to be a dirty war in Vietnam and its associated tragedies and post-war trauma for many National Servicemen and their families, but as social history, as a life-changing experience, a personal upheaval, an identity crisis and amid all the changes, a fun, growing-up time for a bunch of six young men.

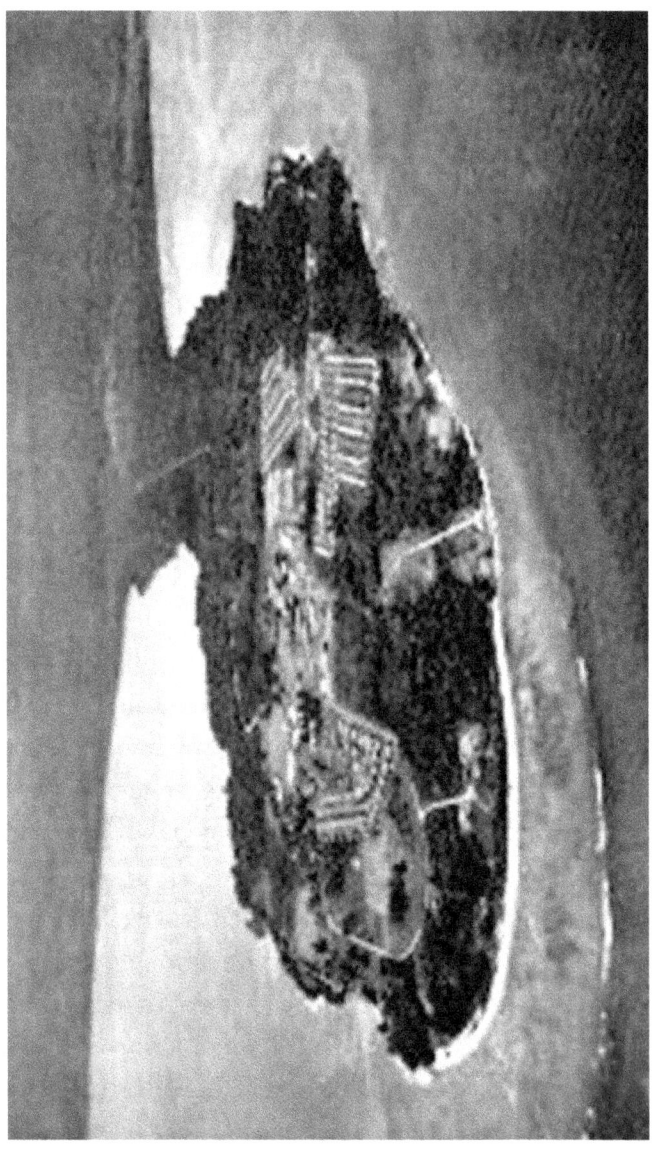

1. Moem Peninsula. TPNG; Sgts Mess on the shoreline at centre-left
Source:http://www.nashospng.com/wp-content/uploads/2011/11/moem-point.jpg

This story is also a counterpoint to big-picture histories that often note but do not provide details of personal dreams, ambitions and opportunities – this is a story of a different National Service, of New Guinea and of young men thrust into a world way beyond their previous knowledge or understanding. The stories are mostly about Wewak, on the far north coast of TPNG, a long way from urban Port Moresby's comforts, diversions and luxuries, and the strict, regulated, disciplined and serious military business at Murray, Taurama and Goldie River Barracks. Moem Barracks the home for the Second Battalion, Pacific Islands Regiment, known as 2PIR, was near the West Sepik town of Wewak, eighteen kilometres away along the coast. The six young conscripts who arrived in mid-1966 had been driving centurion tanks, crewing Bofor anti-aircraft guns, endlessly filing Ordnance requests and dispatches or learning the ropes as a medical orderly. Out of the blue it seemed they were now Sergeants in the Education Corps and looking at a collection of ramshackle *sak-sak* (local sago-palm) material buildings – the Education Centre, Sergeants Mess, sleeping quarters and *haus win*. This was now home for two years.

After being plucked from their expected life as teachers, sent interstate and turned temporarily into soldiers at Recruit Training Battalion at Puckapunyal, Singleton or Kapooka, then Corps training at Holdsworthy, Singleton, North Head, Woodside, Bandiana, or Watsonia Barracks, they were converted overnight into Sergeants in the Army Education Corps, and then in Port Moresby separated from the pioneering cohort of twenty-six Nasho Chalkies sent to Port Moresby, and despatched to the newly constructed Moem Barracks at

Wewak. The Pacific Islands Regiment to which they were posted had begun in 1951 as part of the Australian Army. As twenty-year-olds they understood little of what was happening politically but soon found they were the front line in a policy of preparing the Territory's defence forces for a major role as TPNG headed slowly towards self-government and at some time in the future, decolonisation and independence.

The Education Corps role of the 300 National Servicemen or 'Nasho Chalkies' in TPNG's social and political development and the Australian political and military context for the expansion of the defence forces, has been told in the excellent book by Darryl Dymock, The Chalkies: Educating an Army for Independence (2016). Darryl, one of the early Chalkies, based his book on archival research, his own experiences, and interviews with seventy-three Nasho Chalkies who had served in TPNG. None of the Wewak Six participated directly in his research, thinking their Nasho service was not of interest to a wider public. So, a decade later, what follows is more personal, limited to one small Nasho cohort and concerned with only the inaugural posting of Chalkies to Moem Barracks in 1966-1967. Of the seven original Chalkies sent from Port Moresby to Moem Barracks, one does not appear in the tales covered here, having decided not to be a part of the sporting, boozing, card-playing, darts, surfing and irreverent larrikin life of the other six, or the many trips since, back and forward across the continent for marriages, births, holidays and reunions.

It is also a story about young Australians who grew up not knowing war or living through World Wars and even if there were family members who had served, hearing little from them about their wartime experiences. Only in recent times have the "Wewak Six' shared stories of family involvement in earlier wars. The grandfather of

Helen, Rick's wife, went to France in WW1, suffered a wound in the thigh but survived. Rick has copies of letters, sent from Egypt and France in 1916 by his grandfather Leif to his sister Signa in 1916. Rick's father and father-in-law did active service in WW2 with the latter being trapped behind lines when Singapore fell to the Japanese. Peter's father was a WW11 veteran having served in New Guinea. Jim Kelly, the son of Max's aunty Vera was lost at sea when HMAS Sydney was sunk in 1941. Laurie's father had served in Australian waters in the British Navy in WWII. These stories have a familiar ring to most Australians because serving in other people's wars has a long tradition for Australians going back to the Maori Land Wars in New Zealand, the Boer War in South Africa and on to a series of Asian and European conflicts in the Twentieth Century. When the Wewak Six served their two year's Nasho at 2PIR there was no banter or storytelling of past family connections to military service. It is even more unusual that despite two years as a conscript, no one recalls talking much about National Service over the following fifty years. It was done, and quickly forgotten and was not an episode in life to be highlighted or even mentioned. Sometimes, when asked what he had learned in the Army, Rick answered "to type." This smart-arse answer was not meant to denigrate the sacrifices other men and women had made in past military conflicts. It was only in recent years that the Wewak Six bothered to apply for the four military service medals they had been awarded.

There were twenty-six "Chalkies" sent in the initial posting to Port Moresby in 1966. They were charged with expanding the Army's education program in TPNG. This Army scheme was an inspiration, taking advantage of the expertise swept up in the conscription lottery and meeting a need for development in the Territory. Once posted to Wewak the six had virtually no contact with

Army HQ in Port Moresby, were rarely visited by superior officers and were given very little instruction on what to do. Then in late 1967, replacements started arriving at Wewak and became the next Moem Chalkies – Tony Hedland, Kevin Smith, Kerrie Dohring, and Russell Jenkins. Others served at Moem until 1973 when the Chalkie program was disbanded. A Nasho with Agricultural Science qualifications was also posted to Moem in later years as a *Didiman* (Agricultural Extension Officer) familiarising soldiers soon to be discharged about new crops and agricultural skills.

There is little included here on military matters at Moem Barracks or at Vanimo, a company-level Army base near the border with the former Dutch West New Guinea, then called Irian Jaya and under Indonesian control. Work and life generally were nominally under Army regulations, but the Wewak Six in this story behaved in a rather irreverent un-military manner and enjoyed a much more relaxed type of Nasho experience due to the remote nature of services and facilities on the far north coast, distant from Port Moresby. The context is army life, but it is more about growing up and learning about themselves, about Papua New Guinea and making a modest contribution to improved educational services within the newly expanded TPNG army. It is also a collection of stories about being a Nasho surrounded by "Regs", being an Australian surrounded by Indigenous cultures, communities, and people, and being far from home.

The six young men in this story came from the rural wheat-belt of Western Australia, suburban Perth, Newcastle, Melbourne, and Sydney. They did not know each other before National Service basic training, and the whole group only met for the first time in Wewak. The six became great mates and remain close today.

Happy after completing basic National Service recruit training and then spending a month undergoing further specialist military training, they were posted to Brisbane (Rick), Melbourne (John), Puckapunyal (Pete) and Woodside Barracks in the Adelaide Hills (Bob, Laurie and Max). They were then selected by the Army in an abrupt process lacking a lot of explanation or detail, and virtually overnight sewed on their new Sergeants stripes and flew to Port Moresby. A few days in Port Moresby and they were off again, over the mountainous interior to the far north-west coast. None of the six had any real idea where New Guinea was, let alone Wewak. They enthusiastically started teaching POE and PCOE, (basic English courses) and Social Studies, and quickly adapted to the privileged life of white-masters, albeit Sergeants, overhearing tales at night in the Mess from 'Regs' about the Korean, Borneo and Malayan campaigns of the 1950s and early 1960s, and occasionally a mention of advisor programs in Vietnam.

The strategic and political context for their being in New Guinea was never explained. Mark Dapin notes in The Nashos' that to the average National Serviceman "Nasho' was, "like a series of chaotic incidents triggered by arbitrary orders issued for inexplicable reasons" (Mark Dapin, *Nashos War; Australian National Servicemen and Vietnam*, Penguin 2014, pg. 3).

There were no briefings or detail provided of the wider geo-political and diplomatic events that were drawing Australia into conflicts in Asia. That Number One Royal Australian Regiment, IRAR, the first Australian troops in Vietnam, had been in Vietnam since June 1965 was possibly known but rarely mentioned. The "Chalkies" at Moem were never briefed about how Indonesia had invaded the western end of New Guinea, fought a short war against the Dutch, and had been given approval by the USA and others to take-over in 1963, provisional on a referendum to be held in 1969. They were never told about the wider plans underway in TPNG, driven by United Nations criticism that would lead in 1973 to PNG being given self-government, and two years later independence. In Sepik Province, TPNG, in 1966, it seemed that Australia would always be in charge.

The development of the TPNG Army was clearly of interest to the Australian government during 1966-67, evident when the Australian Minister for Army, Malcolm Fraser, visited Moem Barracks and three Senators also arrived on a look-and-see visit. The Indonesian Ambassador to Australia also visited. His Military Attaché inquired where 2PIR kept its "heavies", meaning tanks. He also noticed coloured flags on a nearby hillside and asked if they were for artillery practice. PIR had neither tanks not artillery. The flags were shipping markers for a forthcoming visit by the naval training ship, HMAS Anzac. The Indonesians were clearly interested in what was going on at Moem Barracks. It was also reported that the Governor of Sukarnopura (the former Hollandia, just over the border) was going to visit 2PIR but this was merely a rumour probably overheard at the civilian Wewak airport.

National Service was a controversial scheme in the years 1965-1973 and is well covered in Mark Dapin, The Nashos' War. He relies on stories from individual Nasho's and presents their army service through a personal life-history approach that focuses on the "reality of the experience for National Servicemen at home and in Vietnam." (The AWM online site has a detailed account of Nasho; Sue Langford, "The national service scheme, 1964-72", at https://www.awm.gov.au/articles/encyclopedia/viet_app).

There were many demonstrations and moratorium marches aimed at ending conscription and getting young men and women out of the mess that was Vietnam, or as we later learnt to call it, the Vietnam War of Independence. Soldiers returning from Vietnam were welcomed by huge crowds, but rumours persisted they had been met with insults and vilified. Involvement in Vietnam was a low point in Australian history, and it helped bring down the ruling Liberal Party government in 1972, replaced by a Labour Government proclaiming, "It's Time". Mark Dapin's account of Vietnam is less about war and more about personal responses and getting on with the job, and here in *Tales from the sak sak* we offer a similar against-the-grain approach which suggests that conscription was a personal success at least for one small group of young men, lucky enough to be posted to a remote army base in the Territory of Papua New Guinea.

Here are some snapshots of Nasho life in TPNG which serve to introduce the main themes of growing up in someone else's country, being promoted awkwardly to Sergeant and being entrusted with a minor educational revolution in the Territory of Papua New Guinea. This is a book about being a Nasho, but also about New Guinea and New Guineans we met, taught, played football with and patrolled with through the mountainous border regions. First, we had to unravel Army routines, then discover New Guinea and then grow up far from home.

THE ARMY
- Saluting, marching, chain-of-command, uniforms and neat cupboards and beds, giving and receiving orders, blindly following what seemed to be inane and unbendable routines.
- After getting a grip on Army life in Australia these routines had to be re-learnt in the Papua New Guinea context. PIR was part of the Australian Army, but the rules and protocols were being applied in a frontier setting.
- Patrolling: being somewhere along the Indonesian border ostensibly on training and mapping exercises was real "Army" life,

dumped in the jungle, tramping about in mud and water over precipitous trails and making incredible traverses of raging steams and deep ravines at Telefomin, Green River, Pagei and Amanab and surviving for weeks on dehydrated rations dropped in by a Cessna or Caribou.
- Mess Dining-In nights; these were compulsory formal events when the tables groaned with food and delicacies sent up from Australia that most had never tasted before. There was a line-up of glasses filled with top wines. The worst rule was that no-one could leave the table heedless of how urgent the need to pee.

PAPUA NEW GUINEA
- Radio: the local Wewak radio station (known as "Radio redwing" for its pro-independence stance) provided a steady stream of mostly C&W classics, but also included indigenous music recorded on cassettes in a burgeoning local studio music scene.
- The Haus Win (open sided building made of local *sak-sak* (woven sago palm leaves and local timbers); this was two metres from the Bismarck Sea, overlooked a fringing reef with crashing waves had a constant tropical breeze and was steps away from cold beer and food. As the locale for home movies, BBQ and pure relaxation, the Haus Win was magical.
- At Moem Point, in the Monsoon season, waves magically appeared over the reef in front the Sgts Mess Haus Win. Pete, Rick, and Max caught small but steep waves, only inches above the jagged corals, until this was banned by the Camp Commandant. Max switched his attention to board riding at nearby Ferok and bodysurfing at Brandi Beach.

- Tok Pisin; English was compulsory on the base, but *tok pisin* had also to be learnt for casual conversations with houseboys and locals in towns, and when out on patrol.

GROWING UP PART 1 (LIFE IN THE SERGEANTS MESS)
- Bingo: Friday nights in the Sergeants Mess where the meaning of "all the threes", "clickity click", "two fat ladies" and "legs eleven" was quickly learnt.
- BBQ: Sunday BBQ in the Haus Win was another Sergeants Mess institution, with a feast of food, notable because Bob insisted on putting tomato sauce on everything.
- 16mm movies; on Saturday nights outdoors in the Sergeants Mess *haus win*.
- 500: this was a card game learnt by all and the source of loud arguments and outrageous bids in the Sgts Mess. "This is serious," "No table talk" and "Slam no trumps" were part of this new language.
- Darts: the reigning institution in the Sergeants Mess was darts. The "regs" (regular Army) Sergeants eventually accepted that Nashos could play darts too, despite being taken aback with the raucous nature of Nasho involvement. The favourite game was "cricket" around the board ending in the need to score multiple bullseyes, and there was also Shanghai, Mickey Mouse and 501.

GROWING UP PART 2 (LIFE IN CIVVIES AND ON DAYS-OFF)
- Music: the 1960s was an amazing era of pop exploration and although banished to the remote nether-regions, LP vinyl records were purchased and played repeatedly along with reel-to-reel cassettes sent up by family and friends.

- Readers Digest: the monthly update on world affairs and with the additional joy of the Readers Digest Condensed Book Club.
- Study: this was only pursued by Rick (who was continuing his university studies) and Bob who seemed to think that everyone

2. L to R: The new NASHO Sergeants, Moem Barracks 1966; Max Quanchi (in Duty Sergeant uniform), Peter Suna, Rick Larsen, (not that short, as he is kneeling) Bob Mason, and John Sweeney (front). Absent: Laurie Bowman who was away with B Coy at Vanimo Camp.

- back home wanted to know about the behaviour of rats in Western Australian wheat silos.
- Squash: this was a sport with a huge following in Australia and the Army had conveniently constructed courts as part of the development of Moem Barracks, although it was only an expatriate pursuit. Bob applied his considerable tennis skills to no effect and Rick and Max became masters of the Moem squash courts.
- Tennis: there were two courts laid out at Moem but never used, to Bob's chagrin. They were given a new life due to Max's determination as Regimental Sports Officer that soldiers would like basketball. They did!
- Wagin Argus and Arthur, Dumbleyung and Lake Grace Express; this local newspaper was sent regularly to Bob by his sweetheart in Kukerin in the WA wheat belt. It was an unexceptional little newspaper, but had the local footy scores, bowling club news, Church times, and agricultural prices. We all read it.

These stories of the Army, New Guinea and life as a twenty-year-old may be unfamiliar to today's readers, but fifty years have now passed and there might be some lessons to be learnt, or life experiences to laugh at from 1966-67. Mostly these are stories about how Nasho affected six young Australian men, and how lives were changed afterwards.

The first account by Chalkies in Papua New Guinea was *Armi Wantoks: Conscript Teachers in Papua New Guinea 1966-1973*, privately published by Ian Ogston, 2004 (paperback, 56 pages).

All photographs and illustrations are by the authors (except where indicated).

.

3. Laurie Bowman, back at Moem, and in his new PIR uniform (but without regulation leather belt and PIR insignia buckle).

CHAPTER TWO

SIX NASHO SERGEANTS

Early in 1966, after being conscripted in the National Service Draft, known as 'Nasho', and doing their basic training, these young men headed off to what they thought would be two years somewhere on an Army base in Australia, or at worst, being posted to Borneo, Malaysia or Vietnam, or 'Nam' as the Americans referred to that war. The government had re-activated the mostly unsuccessful conscription scheme which ran from 1951 to 1956 during the Malayan Conflict. In 1965, lengthened to a two-year term of compulsory military service, possibly overseas, and aimed at increasing enlistment and overall numbers in the regular Armed forces, it was generating confrontation across Australia as protesters and patriots lined up alternatively supporting or condemning conscription and Australia's role in Vietnam. Amid this uproar a quiet selection process by ballot using a barrel full of birth dates took place and the six twenty-year old young men, boys really, went into the third intake of the National Service scheme in January 1966. The Army then selected Nashos who were already teachers or had been undertaking a teacher training course, to be sent to an Australian 'colony' called the Territory of Papua New Guinea, or TPNG. This option had occurred because teachers, students, and apprentices called up in the first two intakes in 1965 had been allowed to complete their year of study or work before heading to recruit training in the third intake in January 1966. There were hundreds of teachers in the third intake. Those chosen to go to TPNG were elevated from their rank as privates and promoted to Sergeant as it was felt, in a racially motivated attitude, that Papua New Guineans would have more respect for 'white' teacher/instructors if they were Sergeants.

In 1966, the Territory of Papua New Guinea was under Australian control. Only twenty years before the two parts of eastern New Guinea had been brought under a single administration, uniting the Australian colony of Papua with the former German colony in the northeast. The German colony had been made a mandated territory of the League of Nations after WW1 and the name "Mandated" had stuck even though after WWII it had become a Trusteeship of the United Nations, again under Australian control. Australia's policies were therefore accountable to both Canberra as an Australian Commonwealth responsibility, and to the UN under its recently formed "Decolonisation Committee" which surveyed annually the transition of former colonies and trusteeships towards self-government and independence. It had been decided by Australia in the wake of a series of regional conflicts - the Korean War, the Malaya War (or Communist Insurgency), Borneo, Indonesia's invasion of the former Dutch colony of West New Guinea, and the Vietnam War - that the future nation to emerge out of TPNG would need an Army to defend its borders, and also enhance Australia's own security. Placing a newly recruited battalion of the Pacific Islands Regiment (PIR) at a newly constructed base at Moem Point near

Wewak was part of this military development, virtually doubling the size of the New Guinea army. As few Papua New Guineans could speak English, learning English became necessary as all orders yelled at soldiers were in English, along with all military manuals. Most recruits and older soldiers could speak either *Police Motu* (common around Port Moresby and in Papua) or tok pijin and could of course speak their own place-talk and perhaps that of neighbouring tribes. Sending Nasho "Chalkies" to TPNG was a brilliantly conceived plan to use Nashos with teacher training or degrees to rapidly bring the English language skills of PIR's soldiers up to a desired "battle-ready" level.

As background to their arrival in TPNG, here is a snapshot of their families, schooling, tertiary studies, and pre-Nasho life. It reveals how unprepared they were to become soldiers or be posted to a foreign country. Let us begin with Robert James Mason or Bob.

Bob was born in Geraldton, Western Australia in 1945 and grew up in humble origins surrounded by a big family. A few weeks after Bob's birth, the Mason tribe took off on a twelve-hour journey inland to a new home in Mt Magnet, a small gold mining town in the Murchison goldfields. Bob's Dad, Taffy, had migrated from Wales to try his luck on the goldfields where he met his wife, Alice, from a farming background but who had moved into Mt Magnet to take up a job with the Council. As they say, the rest is history!! Taffy and his mates built a house from timber and corrugated iron, pleasant in spring, cold in winter and very hot in WA's summer. It was on a mining lease about four kilometres south of town. A windmill drew water from a flooded mineshaft, so the family had an ample and abundant garden. The "outhouse" toilet was down the back. This was a life without modern cons – no power, no running water, no telephone, no sewerage - but plenty of wood for the kitchen stove. Bob's memories of childhood at Mt Magnet are happy and with his four older siblings there was plenty to do, especially on the playground equipment built by Bob's dad in the yard – a slide, swings and a see-saw – and a tennis court constructed from crushed anthills, which was home to many great games by all seven Masons. The rest of Bob's childhood was spent exploring the flat, red soil mulga plains. Sunday was a special day as the whole family drove into the bush to gather firewood, and after a picnic afternoon tea, some hunting and shooting. Bob's Dad was an excellent shot and a keen hunter. Kangaroos were the favourite game but occasionally they bagged a scrub turkey. Yummy – Bob remembers his Mum as a great cook. Then suddenly, it seemed to a young child, the Masons moved to the small farming community of Broomehill in the southwest of WA and found themselves living in an old farmhouse on a 1000-acre property six km out of town.

Bob and his siblings rode into town for school – Bob remembers the classroom as being a brutal experience even for 1951 standards. Out of school, the kids spent hours exploring the lush green paddocks, water filled streams and remnant forests – this seemed a paradise to young Bob as the Southwest had high rainfall in winter. Then just as quickly the family moved again, 100 km further south to the farming town of Cranbrook. This seemed like a good move to young Bob as the house at Cranbook had electricity and, whoopee, running water and the school was across the road. Bob's teacher was a large, kind and caring woman. The Masons stayed for three years and young Bob enjoyed living in town for the first time. Tennis was the favourite after school activity, this time on a bitumen court across the road.

The Sundays collecting firewood, a picnic and hunting continued but without Bob's elder sisters as they had discovered other interests for a lazy Sunday afternoon. This life was disrupted when Taffy gained a promotion to Foreman and Grader Driver at Sandstone, 600 km east into the Gibson Desert. So, in September 1954, off the family went on the road again.

The new house was a converted bakery built of wood and unlined corrugated iron, and without electricity, sewerage, or telephone. The windows were wooden shutters. Bob's Mum never complained and dished up amazing meals for the family of seven, cooked on a "Metters No 2" wood stove. Mum's ginger gems and bread rolls were to die for! The school was a one-teacher school with fifteen children enrolled across grades 1 to 7. Bob's teacher, Mr Vivian, a great bear of a man, was a gentle giant and his lessons were inspirational, and everyone was always well behaved. Bob loved these three years and was inspired to become a teacher himself. Life in Sandstone was remote, quiet, and simple. Weekends were best. Sunday wood gathering, picnic and hunting continued. By this time young Bob was a crack shot. Kangaroos were the main target, for their skins, which had now become valuable. Monday mornings before school was occupied by wire-pegging out the skins in the backyard. Every four months the skins were sent by train to Perth, and this became a little money-winner for the family.

At thirteen years of age, Bob's parents decided against correspondence lessons and despite the expense sent him off to complete his secondary schooling at a boarding school. This was quite a sacrifice for Bob's Mum and Dad. Bob acknowledges the little joys of having a few shillings in his pocket and going to the movies in his spare time at St Christopher's Church of England

Boys Hostel in the town of Northam. There were eighty boys in the Hostel, in five dorms for each of Forms 8 to 12. Hostel life was firm but fair, and stern warnings were numerous. Northam High School was very large for the time, with 900 pupils. It had two-storied classrooms and specialist rooms for physics, chemistry, home science, and technical drawing. It had an "old school tie" atmosphere with attention to school uniforms and regular canning for naughty boys. Bob loved it because of sport. The highlight was winning the local 1960 Australian Rules under-15 inter-school Grand Final. This was a huge experience for a kid from Sandstone where footy (AFL) was a game played mostly by teams of only five or six kids. In Year 10, Bob joined the cadets.

4. Peter Suna, Enlistment photograph 1966.

Bob loved Fridays "On Parade" and even more exciting, shooting at the nearby Army rifle range. In Year 11, Bob joined the Three-Inch Mortar squad and was selected for a specialist Sergeants Course and in Year 12, became the Three-Inch Mortar Sergeant. In 1962, Bob was in everything – the Northam High School cricket team, Australian Rules, field hockey, tennis, and the Cadet rifle shooting teams. The icing on the cake was winning the 1962 Country High Schools AFL grand final. This had involved five games in five days in Perth. In 1963, Bob gained his Leaving Certificate and headed off to Graylands Teachers College in Perth to begin his two-year Primary Teacher training course with 300 other teacher trainee students. Graduating meant passing all twelve subjects so Bob recalls this period as being rather tough. Added to the study was a regular three-week Teaching Practice out in schools. Bob also managed to play in the Graylands basketball, tennis and Aussie Rules teams including an interstate match in Adelaide against SA teachers' colleges. Finally came the dreaded day when the school postings were read out for the graduating students. Robert Mason – Kukerin.

Bob had a little difficulty spelling the name Kukerin and then finding where it was on a map of WA. It was a farming area quite near Cranbrook, where he had briefly lived as a child. As instructed, Bob wrote a polite letter to the Headmaster at Kukerin introducing himself and asking about where he might board. Only Headmasters were provided with housing. Bob did not get a reply, so he headed off into the bush in January 1965 hoping for the best. On arriving at Kukerin the only person at the school was the cleaner who told Bob he had a combined class of Grade of 3, 4 and 5. He gave Bob a key to his classroom. After unloading his scant supply of teaching aids, Bob headed for the hotel. Next morning the Headmaster was a bit off-hand and after showing Bob where the canes were kept, basically said "Get on with it", and for boarding, well just ask around! For a nineteen-year old it was a daunting start to a teaching career. Bob had a fantastic year with his new class and introduced a Friday concert in which talented farm kids danced, sung, and acted. Kukerin was a sports mad town. That suited Bob perfectly. In winter it was Aussie Rules – in an under-performing team who were tossed out of the finals, and in summer it was tennis, played at a remarkably high standard as in most country towns. Then, like his Dad before him, Bob started dating a local girl, Margaret Matthews, from a nearby farm. They enjoyed movies, tennis tournaments and weekends away travelling. Then to shatter this enjoyable life, a letter came in May announcing Bob had been drafted into National Service, starting three months later at Puckapunyal, Pucka for short, in Victoria, on the other side of the continent and far from his sweetheart Margy. Bob applied for a deferment to finish the school year, which was accepted. Some fast talking also sorted out another matter – an engagement. This was celebrated in January just before Bob departed for Puckapunyal. Marriage was to wait. Bob took off for National Service training thinking he might be going to Vietnam and worrying what two years absence might mean to his marriage plans. It might seem to readers that Bob, a crack shot, having already done time in the cadets, and a sporting, fit young Australian might have been eager to join the Army, but his marriage plans and love of rural life were pulling him in another direction.

Peter James Suna or "Black Pete" as he became known by the Nasho Six at Wewak was born in 1945 in Newcastle to Clare and Raymond Suna. He had one sister, Sandra. Pete's father had served in New Guinea in WWII. When his mother became sole carer at a relatively young age, Child Endowment was the only welfare available, so Pete's Mum headed out to work with Pete also taking several after-school jobs. Times were tough. Peter was schooled in the Catholic system by Nuns and by Marist Brothers who often dispensed harsh discipline. Due to his mother's insistence, he completed Leaving Certificate in 1962 and gained a Teacher Training Scholarship to Newcastle Teachers College.

The teacher-trainee allowance was 9 pounds 16 shillings per fortnight so many happy nights at the local Commonwealth Hotel ensued. Sport occupied a key role in Pete's early life. At Teachers College, Peter played Rugby Union, gaining a "Blue" following a 1964 Premiership. Upon graduating from Teachers College in 1965 as a green-around-the-ears nineteen- year-old, Peter's first appointment was to "Dodge City" (aka, Ashcroft High, Western Sydney). This was a challenging introduction to secondary teaching and Pete seriously thought about drafting a resignation letter at the year's end. Then, in 1966, like many others, Pete won the lottery when his birth date marble was drawn.

John Vincent Sweeney was born in 1945 and raised in the inner western suburb of Marrickville in Sydney. The eldest of five children, he recalls life was good. Due to a small backyard, he played a lot in the streets and local parks. His family was not well off, but that did not worry the children as they did not need or expect much. Coming from a Catholic background, John attended the local Parish primary school of St. Brigid's and was taught by the Nuns and then attended the local De La Salle College and was taught by the Brothers. School was a reasonably happy experience and John recalls meeting some good friends. De La Salle

College had a Cadet Corps and being a Catholic school, membership was compulsory, so from his second year at high school, John spent four years in the Cadets, which included a weekly parade after school on Fridays in uniform, plus annual camps and visits to the rifle range. John rose through the ranks to become a CUO (Cadet Under-Officer) and the Adjutant of his Unit. He wore full uniform dress with swords at Passing-Out parades.

5. Peter Suna, finally in full PIR dress uniform, Moem Barracks, TPNG 1966.

John never mentioned this life as a Cadet to the others while at Wewak, or over the next fifty years, as he thought his new Nasho mates would think he was big noting himself. To conform to the ratbag, larrikin approach of the other Nasho Chalkies, he wanted to be equally unmilitary. Neither Bob, Rick nor John, who were Cadets at school never thought this was important to mention while doing Nasho at Moem Barracks.

John's uncle had been the Parish Priest of St. Brigid's church in Marrickville through most of John's schooling. Uncle Pascal had always wanted to be a Missionary and a couple of years before John finished High School, his uncle, now Bishop Pascal, was chosen to take charge of a Catholic Mission in the West Sepik District of Papua New Guinea, based at Vanimo on the northwest coast.

As a reward for passing Leaving Certificate, John's parents sent him to visit his uncle at the Mission and help for a month. Never suspecting he would later be posted to the army camp that he briefly noticed by the airstrip when he flew in and out, John found himself two years later teaching soldiers at this very spot. When John arrived back in Marrickville after his New Guinea holiday he discovered he had been offered a Teaching Scholarship for two years training as a Junior Secondary Science Teacher at Sydney Teacher's College in Paddington, an inner-city suburb. Having few other options at the time, John accepted. Teachers College was wonderful. After so many years in a boys-only school, John finally got to hang out with girls, both academically and socially. Heaven! Soon the two years training was up and with his friends he waited for a school posting. All of John's male friends received postings to Junior Secondary, mainly smaller

Central schools in the Riverina area of NSW. However, it was not John's destiny to commence teaching as he received an official letter declaring, as he put it, "Your number's up". John could not believe his bad luck. He was the only one in his circle of friends and fellow students to win the Nasho lottery. So, instead of heading for a junior secondary science teaching position somewhere in country NSW, he reported to an Army depot for induction into Australia's Armed Service. As it turned out, he did end up in the Riverina area of NSW as his recruit training was at Kapooka Camp, near Wagga.

Laurence Bowman, or Laurie, or "Fingers" as he was known at Moem Barracks, was born in 1945, on a cold day late in winter, the second son to Elizabeth and Larry in a small Scottish coal-mining town called Cowdenbeath, in Fife Shire just north of Edinburgh. His father was an aircraft fitter aboard the British aircraft carrier HMS Victorious in WWII, which had been deployed to the Pacific region and was 12,000 miles away off the coast of Australia. At the end of the war the family moved to another coal-mining town called Gorebridge where another three sons were born, taking the tally to five. Laurie's earliest memories of Gorebridge were of coal mines and dross heaps but also of the surrounding green rolling hills with farms, glens, rivers and burns. Winter seemed long and cold although there was always fun to be had when snow fell. Summer was a delight with the long twilights and warmer weather. Laurie and older brother Bill would spend all the summer holidays hiking, climbing and exploring century-old castles and ruins, not arriving home until late in the evening, ravenously hungry. It was a time when parents did not have to worry about the safety of their kids. Very few people in post-war days could afford a car but the Bowman family was blessed with an old T Model Ford with a canvas covered rear tray. On weekends, weather permitting, everyone including extras, would cram in and head off to some of idyllic spots for a picnic, taking along Mum's superb pastry delights. Great memories! But economic life in post-war Scotland was harsh, especially trying to bring up five growing boys on a small income. Unemployment levels were high and with oldest brother Bill soon to start looking for work, prospects were not good. Larry and Liz made the momentous decision to pack up everything, leaving behind family and friends and immigrate with the boys to Perth, Australia.

On the day in 1957 when Laurie left Scotland it was minus 15C and blowing a blizzard, quite a contrast to the 40C on arrival in Fremantle four weeks later. Eventually the family settled in the Perth suburb of Rivervale where a sister, Mary, was born. Many years later when Laurie was on teacher exchange for a year in England with Lorellyn and their children, Craig and Melissa, he realised how the distance and isolation from family and friends must have been an enormous decision for his parents, leaving everything behind to start a new life for their family, knowing that they would probably never be able to return.

Primary and secondary schooling in Australia for Laurie was unremarkable but heading off to Teachers' College on the other hand was a wonderfully different experience. The atmosphere was more relaxed and sociable, and the men were outnumbered by women five to one. It was there that Laurie met and became good friends with Bob Mason. After two years in college, Laurie was posted to Manjimup Primary school in a timber milling town in the southwest of WA. However, not long into his first term with Grade 4B, the dreaded letter arrived to say that his birthday marble had been drawn in the Nasho lottery and he was to report for a medical at the local hospital. Like most of the teachers drafted, he was able to finish teaching out the school year before entering the third National Service Intake at 2RTB Puckapunyal in January 1966. Laurie had also met and fallen in love with Lorellyn White and they were engaged just before Laurie left to start his recruit training at Pucka.

Rick Larsen, born in Perth in 1945, was the eldest of three sons and recalls having a standard upbringing. Attending an all-boys Catholic school and having no sisters perhaps had led to a skewed, gendered view of life, but school was fine under the tutelage of committed but immature Christian Brothers, who it seemed then, were recruited too young for a life of celibacy, poverty and obedience. Rick says he just kind of 'got on' with things in those school days. There was some pressure to study, but sport played a major role. The military made an early entry into his life when he joined his school's Air Force Cadets. There was no long-term ambition involved but participation in the Cadets was expected by the school and Rick's Dad had been in the RAAF during WW2, so he felt he was keeping a family tradition alive. Being in the cadets was harmless, a bit of a game in some respects. There was lots of paraphernalia with much shouting, some shooting, and some camps with odd rites of passage like applying boot polish to the genitals - of others. Rick does, however, regret an act of minor theft. A lesson was learned: Never break into a Mess supply tent late at night, steal and eat a packet of sultanas, and then take a DC-3 flight [his first ever flight] the next day. It required a XXXL Sick Bag!

There were only limited Year 12 subject choices at a Catholic Boys' School in the early 1970's: English, Maths [I and II], Physics, Chemistry, Geography and Latin and no Manual Arts or practical classes of any kind. While Rick's dad could dismantle a car and put it back together, Rick was more able to solve a pure Maths problem or summarise a book. These school years were cloistered but University came along and helped break down some barriers. At the University of WA, having been good at Maths at school, Rick was placed into a high-achieving State Award winning tutorial group, with girls!! He had never encountered such brainpower, or girls close up. In English classes, Rick's self-esteem was challenged by the Lecturer declaring his offerings "verbose", but psychology classes were more interesting. Socially, Rick enjoyed football, pennant squash and basketball; along with the Young Christian Workers' group and attending many dances where he met his wife-to-be Helen, who finally agreed, on Rick's third attempt, to an invitation for a dance. It was poor judgement when Rick put this budding relationship aside as Nasho days loomed, as Helen was not one to wait around. Rick redeemed himself by having the good sense to re-build the relationship by writing to Helen from faraway Wewak.

Rick says, unashamedly, that he was a 'good' teenager and young adult – very proper but not nerdy; principled but sociable; and tending to be overly reflective. Helen later described Rick as the strong silent type. Rick now considers that he was naïve, including politically, like most young men of this time with his main interests being girls and sport. He was conscientious as a teacher, tried to do well and at the school where he taught, tried to keep the Principal, Mr [always addressed as "Mr"] Richard King, (aka 'King Dick' behind his back), happy. Rick's career aspiration by this time had settled and he wanted to become a Psychologist – a choice first considered at the age of twelve.

Being called up seemed to be part of the normal progress towards adulthood, so Rick maintained a "let's see what happens" approach. It did not come as a shock to Rick when, aged 20 and still ineligible to vote, he was called up. Rick's flat feet were not quite bad enough for Army medicos to reject him, but he was somewhat puzzled when a WAFL footballer was ruled unfit for Army service due to a knee injury – and then continued his WAFL career. There were also reluctant but disappointed conscripts who wrongly believed that eating soap would alter blood and urine tests and would lead to being deemed ineligible. By late 1965, the first ballot and two Nasho intakes had occurred, and Rick assumed he had missed out. Rick had graduated and was essentially minding his own business as a nineteen-year-old in his first year of teaching with fifty-one children in a split Year 5A/6B class in a Perth metropolitan primary school. He could have been in a more remote location, but his Dad's best mate was a Senior Clerk in the Education Department responsible for graduate teacher placement in WA. Having friends in the right place does happen!

The only other male of the same age in the school where Rick taught was Don Barker, an outstanding hockey player. Don arrived at school one day and with mixed emotions, told Rick that a conscription call-up notice had arrived in the mail. Rick's mathematical inklings quickly calculated that his own prospects of being selected had diminished to truly short odds. Going home, where he lived with his parents, Rick's fate was settled as his lucky letter was also waiting. This was the first and last time he has ever been a lottery winner. The 'Call-up' day came, and a group of confused, slightly querulous group gathered at the local Army Barracks, including Don and several guys that Rick knew. Rick carried what he regarded as essentials plus a guitar he could not play; it was his teddy bear equivalent - later to become a problem.

Rick met Laurie and Bob that day for the first time. They had attended a different Teachers' College.

The three met in unusual circumstances. The Army had a penchant for collecting blood samples and Rick tended to faint after blood loss, so when the Army got its millilitres of blood, Rick fainted and fell backwards on to the floor. The sympathy from his three new mates, was brief - a minute – maybe less. Later that day a plane full of Australia's newest recruits from WA arrived at Puckapunyal. They were wonderful fodder for over-exuberant Army instructors or trainers, who seemed to think their success with recruits was being measured on a scale of vitriol.

Pity about that guitar! As Rick got off the bus at Pucka a Lance Corporal screamed, "What do we have here? Elvis Fucking-Presley". This uniformed figure of authority was consumed with his self-importance, and it was probably a line he had used before or, more likely, had heard being used. It seemed somewhat unfair to Rick but unfair became the norm, as everyone soon learned. The message was loud; "Get your arse into gear Recruit, 'cos what I am teaching you will save your life in Vietnam!"

The only Victorian in the Nasho Six at Wewak was Alan Maxwell Quanchi, or Max as he was known, born in 1945, like Bob in a goldfield's town in a rural Australia. Rushworth, a formerly active gold rush town had become a busy railhead for wheat and dairy products from the central Victorian region. Max was the third son to Harry and Grace Quanchi. Harry was of Swiss-Italian descent and worked his whole life in the VR (Victorian Railways) rising to No 1 Station Master at Spencer St (now Southern Cross).

6. Peter's record of the compulsory XRay all conscripts took prior to basic training. Peter had his XRay in November 1965 and entered recruit training in January 1966.

Grace was the daughter of a Scottish pastoralist family from Porcupine Ridge near Daylesford. Max's older brother Valentine (Val) was born in 1929 just before the Great depression, and

Doug in 1934 just after the Depression. To parallel these key periods in Australian History, Max was born a baby-boomer just as the Pacific War came to an end.

Due to his father regularly taking promotion to new postings, Max attended several primary schools. After a year at Swan Hill High School and a move from the Mallee to South Gippsland, his parents decided to stay in one spot so that unlike his two elder brothers, he could finish secondary schooling. Max attended Wonthaggi Higher Elementary School (HES). Although a Technical School, as an HES it also offered a 'professional' stream though Intermediate and Leaving to Matriculation. With just three others and despite doing their subjects by correspondence, Max passed Matriculation, or Year 12 or HSC as it is now known.

During these years he took every opportunity to go surfboard riding, a life-long pursuit he started as a teenager at Cape Patterson. However, as a sixteen-year-old he could not go on to University, so his parents sent him off to Primary Teachers College, where you only needed Form 5 or Leaving Certificate to get in, thinking that after a year, he could switch across to University. It did not work out that way as Max stayed at Primary Teachers College and after two years, graduated as a Primary Teacher and headed to a remote rural school at Tallandoon North in the Snowy Mountains region of northeast Victoria.

This was a lonely experience in a farming community in a one-Teacher school with seven students, but as the year progressed, Max joined local family life, had a lot of fun boarding with an elderly local widow, and became involved in the local tennis and flirting with girls from Wodonga, an hour's drive away where he played Aussie Rules during winter. Max had already won a Best and Fairest Award playing footy and had been drafted by the South Melbourne Swans.

Unbeknown to Max, while he passed his twentieth year quietly in a remote corner of Victoria's alpine region, the Education Department had automatically deferred his National Service so he could finish a year's teaching. So very much out of the blue, a letter arrived in December 1965 that Max was to report to Puckapunyal a month later in January 1966 to join the third National Service intake. That was the end of Max's rural primary teaching career, and his dreams of making it in the AFL.

At Pucka, Max never met the trio from WA, but after finishing basic training he joined Laurie and Bob at the Artillery Training base at North Head, Sydney. The three were then posted to the Light Anti-Aircraft Battery at Woodside, South Australia, from where they were plucked to join the education development project the Army wanted to start in New Guinea. At Wewak, Max, Laurie and Bob teamed up with John, Pete and Rick.

It was a rather mind-blowing transformation for the six young men – from making plans about marriage, footy, tennis, surfing, teaching in remote rural schools or staying in an urban setting, to suddenly be marching, saluting, and following strict discipline and then flying off to another country, hardly known and full of equally unknown indigenous peoples, and then flying even further away to Wewak, wherever that was! Before revealing the experiences faced in the Territory of Papua and New Guinea, as it was then known, the next chapter looks at their basic training and the transition from civvy to army life.

CHAPTER THREE

BASIC TRAINING SALUTING and MARCHING

Basic training for Nashos was undertaken at Kapooka and Singleton in NSW and at Puckapunyal in Victoria so Queenslanders, South Australians, Western Australians, and Tasmanians whose birthday was drawn had to travel interstate. For those from WA this meant an eight-hour flight from Perth to Melbourne followed by a two-hour ride in the back of an army truck up to Puckapunyal. On arrival the new recruits, still dressed in civvies and many wearing only flip-flops were ordered to carry furniture from the QM store to the huts they were to occupy, being abused vocally by Instructors all the way. "Pucka" was cold in winter, hot in summer and was isolated and remote amid farming land between Seymour and Shepparton, north of Melbourne. It had been a training camp for soldiers of the AIF in previous wars and was the major army base in southern Australia. It was chosen as a boot camp for National Servicemen as it already had the basic infrastructure, but new barracks had to be built to accommodate the thousands of Nashos who arrived to undergo basic training.

A lot of time at Pucka was spent on spit and polish – leather belts, boots, brass buttons, rifles and of course learning how to create neat, army-approved beds with hospital folds on sheets and blankets and all edges straight. This was the Army's way of enforcing blind discipline and the following of orders, considered prime qualities of a good soldier. Each day began at 5.30 am. After a shave and shower and a quick clean of the dormitory in preparation for the 7.45am hut inspection there was breakfast. Then each platoon's NCOs carried out the inspection. The day was spent on endless marching up and down, rifle drills, and instructions laden with obscenities and vulgar terms shouted by men who seemed to have come from hell to taunt innocent twenty-year-olds. The level of abuse directed at Nasho intakes was moderated in subsequent intakes. The dreaded call was "clean that SLR son" which meant your Swedish issue, self-loading rifle had to be disassembled, cleaned, and reassembled. This could happen several times a day for unlucky recruits. The SLR was probably the only real danger to our enemies, which at the time was the Viet Cong.

The other standard weapon in the 1960s was the Owen Machine Gun, a light, repeating short-barrel weapon developed in 1940 for close jungle fighting. The magazine held thirty-two, 9mm calibre rounds that made a lot of noise but was ineffective beyond ten to twenty metres. The Owen was notoriously unreliable and either jammed or fired at the slightest jarring. Recruits were allowed to fire 20 single action rounds, and then a burst of 20 automatic rounds from a standing and squatting position. Max bragged in a letter home to his parents that he equal top-scored in his platoon with 26 rounds out of 40 hitting his target, but admitted it was probably a fluke. The M60 machine gun was demonstrated but regarded beyond the scope of safe Nasho training. SLR firing practice, either standing, lying or kneeling at the range, was probably the most exciting part of Basic training for all Nashos as it was regarded as "real" army stuff compared to marching and saluting.

The hand grenade was the third weapon of choice for the infantry, and the pin had to be removed before being thrown as far away as possible. Training took place in a two-metre high, brick-walled embankment. The instructor would tell the squad when to throw and each thrower had to yell, "grenade", hurl the grenade at the target and then fall straight to the ground. Bob recalls an ex-Vietnam instructor being nasty towards a rather hopeless Nasho grenade thrower. So, Bob, having spotted a muddy pool of water, lobbed his grenade in the pool. A great whoosh occurred, and a wall of muddy water sprayed over the Corporal. He was furious and threatened Bob with paying for his laundry expenses. Bob had a familiarity with weapons due to his years in the school cadets, and Max, Bob and Rick had used a .22 rifle mostly for shooting rabbits. Bob's prowess at the rifle range attracted the attention of his NCO Instructor and Bob was mentioned as a possible marksmen or sniper in Vietnam. It was also suggested that Bob would be able to shoot in the Intercompany competitions which comprised weapons assembly and all-terrain shooting with both SLR and Owen Gun. The NCO suggested to Bob he should volunteer for a rifle company – the infantry - after basic training. Bob said he would think it over. At the conclusion of basic training, Bob chose Education Corps, Artillery, Cavalry and Engineers. He was sent to the Artillery.

At night, each platoon was marched to the movie theatre to watch Army instructional movies. Training was basic – meaning order, discipline, constant checks on fitness and an acceptable level of ability with weapons. It was called "basic" because as soon as the ten week course was completed individuals were sent off to further Corps training in the infantry, artillery, tanks, signals, clerical, medical or administrative posts where they could develop more specialised skills. The instructors at Pucka were often men who had already served as Observers in Vietnam and they were scathing of attempts by Nashos to transform themselves into real soldiers. Most recruits soon realised that these insults were not personal but merely the Army's reasoning that shouting, repetition and insult led to improved performance. This repetitive and abusive discipline was often set aside to get a soldier through a test such as target shooting. Bob recalled one recruit who had been a tax office clerk and wore thick coke-bottle spectacles. His attempts at the range consisted of shutting his eyes and pulling the trigger. Bob remembers the Range Instructor handing soldiers on each side of this hapless recruit some extra rounds with orders to fire at the same time at his target. The recruit passed. He ended up as a payroll clerk in the Admin Corps. Max recalled that on his Company's two days at the practice range, out of 280 recruits, only 112 qualified by hitting the target. This was also a costly exercise with 36,000 rounds fired over the two days at one-shilling (10c) a round. Money well spent in the defence of the nation, supposedly.

Basic training involved strange programs such as a half-day spent on 'character guidance', designed to build character, faith, and moral strength, followed by a day of films and discussion groups. Another day was spent on lectures about the Geneva Convention and Codes of Ethics. Basic training also included long route marches and a bivouac on the roads around Pucka with fifty minutes tramping in unison broken by a ten-minute break. Everyone carried their own tent, ground sheet, cooking equipment, rifle and ammunition and this load was probably greater than most recruits had ever toted in their lives. The parched paddocks, stony ground and eucalyptus forest around Pukka were of course poor preparation for what was to come for many Nashos in Vietnam. Of the 15,381 Nashos who served in Vietnam, the death rate for Nashos was an exceptionally high. Of all those Australians killed, 42 percent were Nashos. There are a novel and several documentaries and films, L Montesini, *My life and other misdemeanours*, D McDowell, *Soldier, soldier: A National serviceman in Vietnam* 1969-1970.

Part of the route march involved crawling along hugging the ground to avoid being seen by the supposed enemy. The same degree of enthusiasm was applied to digging latrines. The cross-country trekking also involved mock ambushes, dummy explosives and machine gun fire, setting directions by compass and of course, early morning 'stand-to' in case of surprise attacks at dawn. It also involved going to ground while a rumbling sound from afar gradually increased to a crescendo when a dozen APCs (Armoured Personal Carriers) trundled past to give a sense of being on an actual battlefront. For some lucky recruits, the APCs did a screeching turn around, dropped their back doors and lucky squads were ordered aboard for a free ride home. The APC was the latest innovation borrowed from the USA in the Australian Army and as they had replaced the role once taken by horses for moving troops around, they retained the title "cavalry". Finally, the order would go down the line, "Back to base" and sweeter words were never spoken despite it usually being at least a five- or six-hour route march at a fast pace to get back to Pucka.

One recruit in Rick's hut kept going AWOL and was brought back several times, crying throughout the night until one day he was no longer there. Conscription ballots do not always work! In Rick's view the Army needed trainers who knew how to instruct and educate recruits. Rick was accustomed from his school cadet years to discipline, authority, and obedience; however, the early Nasho recruits often endured irrationally harsh, meaningless activities. The Army was forced, due to the sudden arrival of thousands of Nasho recruits to rely on Nasho Second Lieutenants from the first and second Nasho intakes, who had graduated from the OTC school and were posted to recruit training platoon commanders for subsequent intakes. Rick, through no doing of his own, was almost discharged from Recruit training. His flat feet deemed passable in Perth were further scrutinised, x-rayed, discussed, and subsequently accepted by Pucka's Medicos. Rick's feet were noted in his discharge medical when the Doctor commented, "How did you get into the Army with feet like that? You're going to have trouble with those." Most people know of carpal tunnel syndrome in the hand but not the tarsal tunnel or foot version.

Rick was advised to apply for compensation but received a "not interested" reply from the Army. One recruit had significant acne on his back and at his first medical at Pucka, was told to lay off anything sweet for 2-3 weeks before a re-examination. His subsequent intake of chocolate, Coke and cake meant he failed the test and was sent back to Perth.

Basic training was full of meaningless small tasks and extensive attention to fitness. The PE instructors seemed inexplicably merciless. Nasho recruits came from all walks of life and while some were ready for a military lifestyle due to being in the Cadets at school, others had never experienced anything remotely military. Recognising rank and the appropriate form of acknowledgement was a problem but everyone soon knew the difference between three stripes on the arm (Sergeant) and three pips on the collar (Captain). Max wrote home to his parents he was enjoying camp life and had been elected Hut Captain and Captain-Coach of his Company's basketball team.

At the back of Rick's hut at Pucka was a PE area at the base of a hill with a tree atop – aptly named Tit Hill and in full view. The favourite pastime of one instructor displeased with a recruit's efforts was to order the hapless recruit to pick up a rock, run to the top of Tit Hill, place the rock on the ground, circle it three times and then run back. If not done rapidly ... do it again! In the same vicinity was a stream. Rick's platoon, in full dress with backpack and carrying rifles were told one-by-one to charge at the stream and jump over the running water which was about three to five metres across! Nobody succeeded. Everybody landed in the water and was loudly advised, "A soldier never gets his rifle wet recruit! Do it again!" Rick sorted this out and on his second attempt just before hitting the water, he tossed his rifle on the opposite bank. Bad choice. The instructor barked, "a soldier is never parted from his rifle. Do it again!" Another of Rick's recollections is that he failed a key PE test because he could not swing his ankles up to touch a high pull-up bar. Max also recalls being hopeless at 'chin-ups'.

On Sundays, recruits, in big numbers, marched to the Church of their denomination. Rick wondered how the padre (Army lingo for priests, ministers, and pastors) felt about having a captive audience rather than a voluntary one. One Sundays, as Rick marched towards church, a Lance-Corporal was screaming out

'Left-Rights, Left-Right" accompanied by abuse and chastisement directed at wayward recruits. The Lance-Corporal happened to notice Rick smiling and threatened 'I'll wipe that smile off your face recruit Larsen'. Luckily, the Church loomed near and the Lance Corporal had to tone down his threats and yells.

There were good guys among the trainers at Puckapunyal. On the last night at Pucka the instructors showed their human face and had beers with their training platoon. Rick went to bed early, but his Platoon Sergeant wandered down the aisle of Rick's hut and upended Rick's bed. Rick looked up from the floor and received an unexpected compliment; "Recruit Larsen, we could have made a good soldier out of you if you'd been interested." An accurate comment as Rick really was not interested in being in the Army. During the latter days of training there had been film nights about the various corps of the Army everyone had to apply to join. Rick missed one film, on Ordnance, as he was ill after yet another injection. So, Rick applied for the Education, Psychology and Medical Corps but was dispatched to Ordnance Corps. Rick's selection to Ordnance was announced at a platoon gathering. His confusion at the announcement was overshadowed by a mate learning that he had been posted to ASCO. This recruit must have reached minimum height on recruitment and was still the other side of thin even after twelve weeks of training. When ASCO was announced, he elbowed Rick and whispered, "What's that - the special armed services?" Rick replied – Army Services Canteen Organisation! Although it seemed very un-military at the time it was an important Corps in its own right. The Nation needed everyone.

Perhaps due to his time in the School Cadets, John was awarded the trophy (a small silver cup) as "Outstanding Soldier" in his recruit training Platoon. The Platoon Sergeant, a soldier of many years' service, and not a bad guy compared to others, took John aside for a confidential chat declaring that he thought John had the makings of a good soldier, and should change his selection to Infantry, where he said John was almost guaranteed to serve in Vietnam. Thanking him, John declined. During recruit training, Bob and John had been tagged as suitable for Vietnam, and both declined. John's first pick was the Medical Corps, as it seemed like the knowledge learned might be useful in later life.

Laurie remembers vividly his first day in Nashos. He thought then it was the longest day in his life. The first thing that struck him when conscripts were marshalled into Irwin Barracks in Karrakatta WA, was how many of the guys were mates he knew from Teachers' College days. One was a close mate from Graylands Teachers College, Bob Mason, but whom Laurie had rarely seen since graduating. Another of Laurie's mates, Don, introduced him to a colleague that Don had been teaching with in Perth, Rick Larsen. Laurie did not see Rick again until later that year in New Guinea. The rest of the day was a bit of a blur with lectures, medicals, meetings, and lots of sitting around, followed by a sleepless overnight flight from Perth to Melbourne. After they got to Puckapunyal and were assigned to a platoon; half a day was gone. The rest of that afternoon was spent queuing up for uniforms and kit, more needles, bedding, haircut, and hut allocation. By lights-out at 9.30pm that night, when everyone finally had a chance to rest, it felt like they had been in the army for a week.

Pete recalls exactly that his basic training commenced on the 2nd February, 1966 at 3RTB (3rd Recruit Training Battalion) at

Singleton, NSW. This was followed by specialist Corps training with the 1st Armoured Regiment at Puckapunyal as a Gunner/Signaller. Training in Centurion tanks involved attacking old car wrecks with AP (Armour Piercing) and HE (High Explosive) shells.

During basic training for Nashos a few recruits had been selected and put through a day of physiological and psychological tests to see who was suitable for command and promotion to Officer rank as Lieutenants. Max was chosen for the OTC trials but mostly stood back and watched. He was sent back to recruit training. Rick was also chosen for the trials conducted by a panel of Officers and a Psychologist trying to identify leadership and Officer rank potential. The evaluation involved a written test, an interview and team exercises solving hypothetical problems. This involved a group of about ten prospects, an imaginary stream that needed to be crossed with three planks, four tyres and three bits of rope. The Instructors stressed the stream must be crossed quickly and efficiently as military danger loomed, so ideas were needed, verbalised, communicated to the others, and acted upon. Rick decided to take a back seat and observe while others pushed their way to the front. About 300 Nashos were whittled down to 160 aspirants, with about 60 doing the final tests. Some Nashos served their two years as Officers, including Max's school and Teachers College mate, Geoff Levy. At the closing interview Rick was asked why he took a back seat and he respectfully explained why. He was then asked a few questions;

Officer: "Are you interested in Officer Training recruit?"
Rick: "If I was selected what are the chances that I'd be posted to Infantry?"

Officer: "Very high."
Rick: "And what are the chances of being sent to Vietnam?"
Officer: "Very high."
Rick: "Thank you, but I'm not really interested."
Interview ends.

At the end of the ten-week basic training, it was time to select the corps or type of military service where Nashos wanted to spend the rest of the two years. Max reported to his parents that he had met an ex-Teachers College mate, who had become a regular Army Captain in the Education Corps, who advised Max not to apply for Education Corps. Max cannot remember what he chose and ended up in Artillery.

It seemed to the six, now fully trained recruits, that the remainder of their two years would be spent somewhere in Australia, and that Nasho would turn out to be OK.

7. Three gunners at firing range (Laurie, Max and Bob). Victor Harbour, South Australia, June 1966

CHAPTER FOUR

CORPS TRAINING and then to PORT MORESBY

Advanced Artillery training for Nashos was undertaken at the School of Artillery at a barracks situated on North Head in Sydney. North Head was a dream posting overlooking Sydney harbour on the landward side, the Pacific Ocean to the East and the popular resort of Manly to the north. Soldiers had a private, but shared cubicle which was a pleasant change after the all-in, platoon-size dormitory housing at basic training. The floors glistened and all brass fittings and windows and window ledges were kept spotlessly clean under the keen eyes of NCO Instructors. The parade ground was red pumice which crunched when marched upon. The food was excellent and served in two sittings. Bob and Laurie were joined by Don Barker, Rick's teaching mate from WA, and on their free nights they would wander down to Manly for a few cold beers at the Pacific Hotel. Life in Sydney, Australia's biggest city, was exciting with Bob and Laurie enjoying many excursions with family and friends from WA who now worked nearby. Bob and Laurie had quite a few sessions at the

8. Max and Laurie, Woodside Army base, SA, June 1966.

Canopus Room at the Manly Hotel. At North Head they met Max who would go on to join them at 111 Light Anti-aircraft Battery in Woodside in South Australia. While at the Artillery School, Max played Aussie Rules for North Shore and in a representative Army versus Navy game. The Manly ferry to Circular Quay was utilised many times and the notorious Kings Cross visited, but only for a Shirley Bassey concert at a famous club.

Training at North Head was initially on the nearly obsolete 40mm anti-aircraft Bristol Bofor, a relic of WWII. The Bofor used armour piercing shells shaped like a long soft drink bottle with a 30cm brass casing.

It also fired tracer and explosive shells and had an impressive rate of 40 rounds per minute and could be fired in automatic or in single fire manual mode.

It had advanced hydraulics and a squad of six with three stationed on the carriage feeding in magazines, but was practically useless against the high-altitude, sub-sonic and jet aircraft developed after WWII. In Vietnam, they were also used with barrels parallel to the ground in a strafing role against advancing infantry. After the basic Bofors course was completed, there was a chance to go on to Signals training. Bob and Max missed out but Laurie and their new mate Bronte Williams from Streaky Bay, SA, were selected for additional courses.

Eventually Bob, Laurie, Max, and Bronte were reunited when posted to the Light Anti-Aircraft Bofor Battery at Woodside Barracks in the Adelaide Hills. Max had driven his car overland to Adelaide alone. He wrote to his parents that the Army offered a liberal $26 per diem for the trip. Army regulations were that no passengers could be taken when making long car trips, so Laurie and Bob took the train, enjoying the luxury of a sleeper paid for by the Army on the interstate service via Melbourne to Adelaide. The luxury continued at Woodside with each gunner being given a private room, and a strip heater to combat the freezing conditions at night in the Adelaide Hills. The temperature fell so far at nights that water pipes on the outside of buildings froze. The luxury also extended to the catering which Bob enthusiastically attacked with sauce bottle in hand.

Woodside was rumoured to be a temporary posting as the Battery was said to be destined for the British air force base at Butterworth in Malaysia and then on to Vietnam. Every year there was a rotation of gunners to Malaysia even though the Communist uprising in Malaysia and the Indonesia-Malaysia confrontation were now over. When invitations to volunteer for Butterworth were announced, Bob thought about it but did not put his name down, heeding his dad's advice: "Never volunteer for anything".

At Woodside, the thirty or so gunners in the Anti-Aircraft Battery were a distant second in pecking order to the thousand infantrymen of the 2nd Battalion AIF, also stationed at Woodside. The Artillery Battery's duty was at the front gate which luckily meant avoiding the long cold nights of patrolling the grounds and perimeter fences. Gate duty involved a rotation of 2 hours on and then four hours sleeping in a warm guardhouse. Most of the infantry were local South Australians. When they took leave at weekends the camp was quiet, and the gunners had open use of facilities.

Trips to Adelaide were made regularly for shopping, movies, and football. Max was not impressed with Adelaide in the 1960s, telling his parents, "It is quite funny … Adelaide on a Saturday morning is only about as crowded as Colac, nothing like Melbourne". He added that it had no tall buildings like Sydney and Melbourne, but he did note he was seeing a fair bit of Australia, from North Head and Sydney, across the outback by road and now Adelaide. Max wrote home that it was indeed true: "See the world for sixpence, Join the Army". After receiving glowing letters from Nasho mates posted to Queensland, NSW and Victoria,

Max suggested to his parents that "National Service isn't all that bad now to some of the blokes who grizzled when they first joined".

Sport was back on the agenda. Max organised an Army team to play in a weekday football competition down in Adelaide and Bob and Laurie joined in. Max arranged for some gunners to play in the local Adelaide Hills weekend footy competition while he tried his luck with Sturt in the SANFL where he had to play under an assumed name in a feeder competition until his interstate transfer arrived. The daily routine on base revolved around the Bristol Bofor with continuous drilling in preparation for the rumoured posting to Malaysia and Vietnam. Finally, a live firing was planned. A few Bofor were towed down to the Army's live firing range at Victor Harbour. Firing had been part of the training at North Head, but only using blank rounds fired at a drone being towed down the Sydney coastline by a light plane. At Victor Harbour it was live ammunition. By using tracer rounds the Instructors could note hits on the drone and see how effective the gunners were at loading and re-loading under the pressure of an imagined attack. After setting up camp near Victor Harbour, at Waitpinga, Bob, Laurie and Max pranced around the firing range dressed in jungle fatigues trying to look like real gunners. Meanwhile, with so many trained teachers in the early 1966 intake, Army planners realised that they had a huge untapped ready-made teacher trained resource which they could send north, to teach in TPNG's newly expanded Pacific Islands Regiment. Bob, Max, Laurie and Mick Barrington, a teacher from NSW, were picked it seemed to them, at random from the third Nasho intake for interviews for this job.

9. Peter's medical record indicating cholera shots prior a few days prior to leaving Australia and then subsequent checks by the RMO at 2PIR.

The Bofor shooting exercise at Victor Harbour had not even started when a staff car pulled up and an Officer informed the Battery's CO that Bowman, Quanchi, Mason and Barrington were to gather up their gear and go to Adelaide railway station to catch the night train to Melbourne.

All they were told was it was for interviews for a posting to the Territory of Papua New Guinea as teachers in the Army Education Corps. The interstate overnight train from Adelaide to Melbourne in those days was a sit-up redeye experience. On arriving at Spencer Street station, the group were driven to St Kilda Road Army Barracks where a meal and time for a shower was provided. Individually the four gunners went in for an interview with an array of brass lined up on the other side of the table. The atmosphere was friendly and standard questions were asked about teaching background, sport and hobbies before posing the big question – "Why do you think you should be selected to go to New Guinea?" This was a ridiculous question as no one had any idea where New Guinea was, what the Australian Army was doing up there, and why they wanted Nashos who had teacher training. The rest of the day was free, so Max borrowed his Dad's new Holden and the boys enjoyed a tour of the nearby Mornington Peninsula. That night it was back to Adelaide on the overnight interstate train. They had no idea what the trip and interviews were about but had a great time in Melbourne and returned none the wiser. Back at Woodside the Battery was already busy cleaning the gear used at the live firing and the strange trip to Melbourne was quickly forgotten.

Laurie, Bob and Max were later called to the CO's office and informed they had missed out on New Guinea and that Gunner Barrington had been selected for promotion to Sergeant in the

Education Corps and a posting to Port Moresby. That night they all celebrated in the mess and wished Ken the best of luck in his new role. First thing next morning, all were summonsed back to the CO's office and told there had been a mix-up and it that it was Bowman, Mason and Quanchi who were going to New Guinea and Barrington had missed out. What a stuff-up! Mystified but excited the three went home on leave to WA and Victoria for a few days and then reported back to Woodside.

A few days later, Ken Barrington was ironically on Guard Duty at the Woodside gates as the trio headed for Adelaide airport and the flight to Port Moresby. After another round of injections and then checking in their luggage, they spent the rest of the day wandering about Adelaide and watching the box-office hit movie "Dr Zhivago". Before they left for PNG, the new Sergeants had their first taste of how "Regs" would react to Nashos being given the rank of Sergeant. At Woodside Camp regular Infantry Sergeants refused to recognise their new rank or allow them to visit the Sgts' Mess. It was early days still in Nasho, and some 'Regs' clearly could not accept upstart Nashos being promoted so easily. There would be more of that.

Rick's Corps training was at Bandiana Barracks near the Victorian-NSW border town of Wodonga where he learnt typing and filing, and of course how to shoot, duck and hide, and how to turn the soldier button "on" and how to switch to "Army Off". After ten weeks, Rick was posted to 1BOD, Base Ordnance Depot, at Enoggera in Brisbane. Rick shared a room with another Nasho and worked office hours, starting, and finishing on a siren (including lunch, morning and afternoon breaks) while extracting and re-filing multi-digit cards as stock numbers were adjusted for bolts, screws, nails and other Army equipment as required. A

Year 12 education, minimum, was supposedly a pre-requisite for this job. Misfiling a card required a manual search - as boring as the proverbial bat-shit. This was office drama in a military setting. Rick did not complain, did his job, watched the clock, counted the days, and bought a Renault 750, same as the car he had back at Teachers' College. An Adjutant approached Rick one day at his filing cabinets [that is a big plural] and advised that the Army was looking for trained teachers to post to TPNG and asked whether Rick would be interested in going to Sydney for an interview. Rick had packed up his desk before the Adjutant had finished the question.

John's Medical Corps training was at Healesville, in the Dandenong Ranges outside Melbourne. The accommodation was in tents and it was very cold. Outside each tent were buckets of water, in case of fire and for most of John's time there, in the morning the water in the buckets were frozen solid. (The same thing was happening to Bob, Laurie, and Max in the Adelaide Hills). On a visit to Melbourne, John attended his first live game of Aussie rules, Carlton versus St. Kilda and it was only in later years that he realized that he had seen some of the giants of the game. John's choice as best on ground was a nuggety Carlton player called Ron Barassi and St. Kilda had a fairly good player named Darrel Baldock, later to be idolized in the Moem Barracks Sergeants Mess by Bob "Wriggles" Wriggley who features several times in later tales. After ten weeks of Medical Corps training, John was posted to No 2 Camp Hospital at Ingleburn, an outer area of Sydney. There did not seem a lot to do in the Medical Corps, so days were spent mostly trying to find ways to fill in time. Without warning, John was told to attend an interview for trained schoolteachers, who were to be posted to TPNG to help in the education of soldiers in the Pacific Islands Regiment. At the interview, John mentioned that he had been to TPNG for a short time, two years earlier.

It also turned out that one of the interviewing Officers had served at Vanimo Army base and met John's uncle, so John thought that did not hurt his chances of escaping the Medical Corps and returning to TPNG. Shortly after, with his newly sewn on Sergeant's stripes, John was off to Port Moresby. One of the last of the twenty-six initial Chalkies to arrive at Murray Barracks, he was posted to 2PIR in Wewak. Three days in Port Moresby made John glad he was going to Wewak, not far from his Uncle, Bishop Pascal Sweeney at Vanimo.

Pete remained with the Armoured Corps until July when he was taken to Watsonia Barracks outside Melbourne and interviewed with others by a panel of Colonels and Brigadiers regarding a transfer to the Education Corps in TPNG. A week later back on the firing range, out of the blue, an APC (Armoured Personnel Carrier) roared in and escorted Pete back to camp informing him to pack his gear for a return to Watsonia the very next morning. There Pete met six others who had been selected for New Guinea. After multiple vaccinations they were told of their next assignment was sewing. With a mixed degree of competency, they sewed on Sergeant's stripes for a very apprehensive introduction to the "Snake Pit", aka the Watsonia Barracks Sgts Mess, at 5pm that evening. Any animosity was thwarted with an address by the RSM welcoming Nashos into the Army and his shouting of beers for all. Pete was awarded six days' leave with orders to return to Watsonia for more vaccinations.

The three from Adelaide flew from Adelaide in an 'Electra', and recall they did manage to sink a few in its "lounge" area until ordered back to their seats! In those days, the commercial flight to Port Moresby by the amazing new Boeing 727 "T-jet" involved refuelling stops in Brisbane. Peter recalled it was his first flight ever. The shock of disembarking on a rather humid Port Moresby morning, in winter uniform, was made even more memorable by a serious "hangover" state. When the plane doors opened for Bob, Laurie and Max, a rush of Port Moresby's hot tropical air flooded the plane and three slightly inebriated young Nasho's stomachs started to move. Max rushed off and vomited behind the hangar while Bob made it as far as the toilets in the Arrivals Lounge. Laurie was feeling a little shabby but kept his stomach down. It was not a good start.

An Education Corps Officer drove them through the dry, hilly suburbs of what appeared to be a rough and tumble shanty town and finally to Taurama Barracks in the suburb of Boroko. Max reported home to his parents, using racist language in common use at that time; "Natives everywhere and not doing anything. They are a pretty lethargic lazy race it seems. No go at all ... as for the Territory it is a time of fast change and English speaking, and education, are prime requisites if they are going to get there". Max reported home that "they really need us up here, so we have been told ... we are definitely the shining stars". The transport Officer was surprised the ex-gunners were dressed in heavy winter khaki rather than in PIR tropical uniforms of shorts and short sleeves and that Bob, Laurie and Max were not displaying their Sergeant's stripes. This had been another stuff up caused by the Woodside Payroll office not providing Pay Books. Army rules were – no Pay Book, no issue of uniforms. So, the three gunners arrived at Port Moresby's Taurama Barracks in full AIF gunner's winter gear, long pants, long sleeves and thick serge and flannel uniforms. The CO of the Education Corps at Taurama was shocked when told the official attitude at Woodside had been that gunners could be Sergeants in New Guinea but not on the Woodside patch. "Typical bloody Infantry" was the response at Taurama Barracks. PIR tropical gear was issued but only because the CO overlooked Army rules. Stripes were issued quickly, and an officer's wife kindly sewed on the stripes. Finally, Bob, Laurie and Max felt they really were Sergeants.

A Sergeant is often referred to as the rock on which an Army is built due to their role in translating commands from above (Officers and Field Command) down to the other ranks (ordinary soldiers) at the bottom. Sergeants were the direct face of the Army at the operational unit, the platoon of around 25 soldiers. The rank of Sergeant therefore earned respect from both officers and ordinary soldiers. The path to gaining the rank of Sergeant was slow, often ten years or more, and based on both performance and length of service. Promotion to Lance-Corporal, then to Corporal was quick but the next step to Sergeant was more difficult. Sergeants could then move further up the NCO (Non-Commissioned Officer) ranks to Staff-Sergeant and then Warrant Officer I and II, and CSM (Company Sergeant Major) and at the top of the NCO pile, to RSM (Regimental Sergeant-Major). Group 6 Education Sergeant's pay was higher than a newly graduated teacher's pay back home. Laurie quickly noted this put him on a pay scale equal with the highest teaching salary for a classroom teacher in WA at that time. Not bad, he reckoned for his first year out of college!

It seemed to Rick when he arrived in TPNG, that he was now equal in Army terms to the status to the "God Sergeants" of Pucka days. As well as being paid more than they were as teachers, Rick considered it a bonus because they had accommodation, free food, medical and other perks to boot. Things were looking up! Rick had arrived in Port Moresby alone and spent a few days waiting before being posted to Moem Barracks. The north coast posting appealed to Rick as he thought the city and suburbs of Port Moresby, on first impression, were unattractive. Rick reasoned that if he had to serve two years in the Army, then Wewak ("Moem" was not used as a name at this time by the Nasho Six) seemed to be the best posting. With hindsight everyone agrees that going to TPNG and then to Moem Barracks was a lucky break.

Laurie, Bob, and Max spent a day at Taurama Barracks looking over the courses to be taught by the newly arrived Nasho Chalkies, followed by a tour of Goldie River, the boot camp for recruits into the PIR, and then to Bomana WWII Memorial Cemetery on the outskirts of Port Moresby. This was an emotional experience when it was realised that many of the graves on the beautifully manicured lawns and garden beds were for soldiers who were boys younger than the Nasho group. The thousands of white marble headstones maintained by the Commonwealth War Graves Commission left the Nashos with a lasting sadness of the cost of war. (There are also cemeteries at Lae, Samarai and Rabaul, as Australia buries its dead in the country in which they fall, unlike the Americans who take all bodies back home to the States.)

After a daunting and uncomfortable formal dinner in the Sergeant's Mess, the initial group of twenty-six Nasho Chalkies were allocated randomly to Taurama, the Goldie River recruit training camp, Moem Barracks or Murray Barracks HQ. Bob was initially posted to Taurama but luckily a Nasho posted to Wewak was a keen rugby player back in Sydney and wanted to play in the Port Moresby A Grade competition. A swap with Bob was suggested and Max approached an Education Corps Major on Bob's behalf and was told permission had to be gained from the Colonel. Max organised a meeting and did most of the talking and to everyone's surprise the top brass agreed. The three ex-North Head and ex-Woodside mates were off together to Moem Barracks. Bob shouted several rounds in the Sergeants Mess that night.

A day of leave followed so a nearly brand-new Holden was hired, Max recalled for the princely sum of $12, and Max, Laurie and Bob took off into the back streets and windy, dusty roads of Moresby and its suburbs. Typically, they took no notice of the time and returned the car extremely late at 9pm and were punished by having to pay for a taxi back to Taurama Barracks. The next day it was off to Moem Barracks at Wewak, but no one had any idea where it was or what their role would be. Max wrote home he was glad to leave Port Moresby; "it is a very disappointing place and I'm not sorry I'm going to Wewak, although it sounds like the end of the line".

CHAPTER FIVE

LIFE AT MOEM BARRACKS

In the 1960s the flight from Port Moresby to Wewak was in a propeller driven DC-3, the former work horse transport plane of WWII. The flight went up over the massive central cordillera and then descended to Lae on the north coast for refuelling, followed by a two-hour flight up the Markham Valley and over the Sepik River and then westward following the coast to Wewak. The welcome party at Wewak for Laurie, Bob and Max was a smartly uniformed Education Corps Lieutenant who drove the three new Sergeants out to Moem Barracks. The first disappointment was when they passed by the brand new three-story barracks for the soldiers but were dropped at a collection of weathered, low *saksak* buildings made from local materials with thatched sago palm leaf walls, corrugated iron roofing and bamboo shutters. The bonus was a fringing reef fifty metres offshore that created a lagoon right along the beach fronting both the Sergeants and Officers Mess. New Guinea seemed like picture book. Indeed, in Max's first letter home to his parents from Moem barracks he declared, "It is a virtual paradise. Lush green jungle backed by hills on a peninsula with green sea on either side. It is just like the pictures you see of Tahiti".

Moem barracks was best described as a work-in-progress and was in the process of being expanded so the lines of canvas tents for soldiers were being replaced with new brick, glass, and steel dormitories. There was separate Aussie-style housing for officers and married OR's (or Other Ranks, locally enlisted personal – LEP). The married Australian Officers and NCOs houses were just inland from the Mess while the married Papua New Guinean NCOs and ORs lived in newly built married quarters on the other side of the camp. The Wewak Six came as single men. Later arrivals with wives were allocated to relatively luxurious new three-bedroom homes in the middle of the base. The bonus for living in the old Sergeants Mess was an absolute beach front with a million-dollar view.

10 The new buildings, Moem Barracks, late 1967.

Each 'donga", or bedroom, was small but roomy and breezy with bamboo shutters and only separated from the Bismarck Sea by ten metres of gravel pathway. The ablutions - the shower and toilet block – were in a separate *sak-sak* building out the back. There were no glass windows. Everything inside the donga was covered in dust from the millions of borers which tried to eat their way through the untreated timber of the exposed beams. The roof and walls also were home to myriads of geckos. Each donga had a ceiling lined with calico and tarpaper to stop rat droppings from landing on the desk, chair, bed with mosquito net and wardrobe. Nights were noisy, mostly from rats scampering around in the tarpaper lined ceilings. Two sergeants shared a common doorway. This was the single Sergeants quarters.

One bonus of living in the older *sak-sak* single Sergeants quarters was not having to clean rooms or wash clothes as all cleaning, washing and general maintenance was done by a haus-boi, a local civilian hired by the Army, with a little top-up payment from each Sergeant. They were older men, not boys.

There were no female service personnel, Australian or Papua New Guinean at the Moem camp. Papua New Guinean female officer cadets were not inducted into the PNG Defence Forces until 2013. In 1966, only the wives of a few Australian NCOs and Officers were on the base. Aussie Nuns and Sisters at the local churches and nurses and doctors at the Wewak hospital were rarely sighted. The absence of women was the cause for much teasing, frustration, and over-exaggerated machismo.

The Sergeant's Mess fronted a small beach and reef passage and once the monsoon arrived there was four months of rather risky

11. Rick coming out of ablutions block, Sgts Mess, 1966.

body surfing. Perhaps it was not perfect for a late-night naked body surf, but it was irresistible. Pete, Max, and Rick had grown up bodysurfing and this was too good an opportunity to pass up. There was also surf near the Mission Point at Vanimo. (Today, there is a well-known surfing resort there, Vanimo Surf Lodge).

Another board spot was at Boram halfway between the camp and Wewak town, where a small set of waves rolled over a reef during the monsoon season. There were no beach patrols. By using the Army's aluminium runabout, the Nasho Six soon realised they could scoot down the coast at weekends with a few surfboards and surf the break at Ferok, a few kilometres east along the coast where a river entered and had built up sandbanks across the river mouth. This meant the waves broke further out and rolled across the banks, perfect for boards. Bob learned to stand up and for the first time surfed some small waves. Brandi beach was nearby and was a black sand beach for bodysurfing, with two to three metre dumpers that crashed straight on to the beach. This was an exhilarating ride but required a tumble turn back under the wave to avoid being crushed on to the sand. Brandi was lined with coconut palms and behind was a freshwater lagoon perfect for a post-swim dip.

The sleeping quarters for Sergeants were twenty metres from the Mess Dining Room and Bar. The food was remarkable as the quality far surpassed what the young Nashos were used to back home. Sitting down for three course meals, waited upon by soldiers on roster for kitchen duties was slightly formal but the variety was amazing, and paid for by Australia with seemingly no attention to cost. Bob soon made himself the King of the Tomato Sauce Bottle. The story of Bob's savvy in meal ordering, which the rest teased him about, was on display at the gourmet weekend barbeques. Bob would pick the eye out of magnificent pork chops and leave the rest of the chop, he said, for others to enjoy. Laurie recalls a more senior NCO seeing these remnants on the BBQ and demanding, "Who did that and left this here?" Bob still has a healthy appetite!

The tucker in the OR Mess was far more basic and centred around staple foods: pork, fish, chicken, taro, sweet potato, sago, rice, local fruits and coconuts. The way food was served was also more basic, but the quantities provided left no soldier wanting.

12. Rick at the freshwater creek on the beach walk to the Catholic Mission, Vanimo 1966.

The newly arrived Nasho Sergeants made lots of mistakes and there was plenty of hostility towards their rapid promotion and it was very much "us versus them" when they first appeared in the Sergeants Mess at Moem. Possibly this was the reason the six young Nashos became such a close-knit group. Camp life was good for a bunch of twenty-year olds and friendships were made with "Regs" and Papua New Guinean NCOs once the initial frostiness wore off. John arrived last and met the five guys who were going to be his friends for life, although no one realised that at the time. Looking back now on those first few weeks after arriving at Moem, John agrees the Nasho Chalkies were a rude shock to the existing regular Army members of the Sergeants Mess. These "Regs" had been in the Army for many years and taken a long time to reach the ranks of Sergeant and Warrant Officer. They were accustomed to a staid and conformist Mess regime, a quiet drink after dinner and chatting until they retired to bed.

Looking back, John recalls the six new arrivals were loud as only twenty-year olds can be. They played darts and were loud, and they played cards and were even louder. They mixed with the Pacific Islander Sergeants, which the "Regs" did not. The peaceful and routine lives of the "Regs" had come to an end and most did not like the new atmosphere. On the positive side, John recalls the Nasho Six always played with the children of the "Regs" when their families came down to the beach. Gradually peace prevailed and both sides learnt to share the Mess on amicable terms. Most of the European NCO's were probably late 30's or early 40's and some were "really old", like their newly acquired AFL football-loving mate, WO Bob Wriggley. The Nasho sergeants also gravitated to the newly promoted and youngish Papua New Guineans and some close friendships developed. All six of the Wewak Chalkies fondly recall a fellow basketballer and AFL footballer, a WO2 from Buka Island, Peter Mamare.

Rick contacted Peter's son, Fabian Mamare in 2019 and received the following letter (reprinted with Fabian's permission.)

"Dad passed on in 2003. I was at a work site in the Southern Highlands Province when it happened and so I travelled the next day. I buried him next to his father, there hours after arriving. A massive stroke I was told! Between 1968 and 1970 dad spent a lot of time down South in Australia. Mum, my big bro and I spent months on end living

by ourselves at the Moem Married quarters while he was in Australia. I do not know when he attained his certificate in teaching in Australia. I believe he was the first National in the Army to attain this qualification. On another occasion he returned with the Australian SAS and parachuted in to open the Cape Wom memorial, again the first National to jump and land on PNG soil. He replaced RSM Manli after Paulus left the Army to contest the National elections. We left Moem barracks in late 1974 when Dad was transferred to become the RSM at Goldie River and we were there until 1980. He was then transferred as RSM at Lombrum Naval base. He served in the Vanuatu conflict (ed., the so-called Santo Rebellion just prior to Vanuatu's independence) but was offshore on one of the patrol boats I was told. He retired after the Rebellion in Vanuatu. Dad was the Secretary for our Community-level Government from 1982 to 1988 after leaving the defence Force in 1981. After the Bougainville Crisis (ed., 1988-1998) Dad was involved heavily in the land mediations in all North Bougainville and he remained the Chairman and Land Mediator until his passing. He trained a lot of the current Magistrates when they entered the Law and Justice sector at the community level. His involvement with sports and youth was his passion and he mentored and motivated youth to perform their best whether it was basketball, volleyball, or soccer. From 1988, until his passing he was a Magistrate and became the Chairman of all the Magistrates in our constituency. Dad told me stories of his patrols and what I remember most is the chocolates from his ration packs - those were the best. I heard a lot of stories regarding the resentment by the old war-dog NCOs to you guys, the Nashos straight from teacher training and becoming overnight Sergeants. Anyhow you came to do a job and you did it successfully. I would love to have a copy of your book if you ever have it published. I know it will be an awesome read. I miss Dad very much. He was respected by his peers at home and always involved with the community, but to me he was simply, Dad. A friend to all, and enemy to none sort of a person."

The authors sincerely thank Fabian for sharing these memories.

The Nasho Six from Moem regret that they did not do more to continue these open and friendly connections after they returned to Australia, although Peter Mamare did send Max some advice on the need to get married.

On one occasion Bob returned to his donga to find a huge sea turtle had wandered in from the beach just ten metres away. With the help of some ORs and corporals the weighty turtle was relocated back in its watery abode.

Although racism in the Camp was frowned upon, local and Australian salaries were markedly different and there were other distinctions such as local married soldiers who had far more basic accommodation than married Australians. Despite the military and social barriers, the Nasho Six made friends with local colleagues including Peter Mamare, Paulus, Peter Anasis, Robert Iei and others through sport and shared interests.

An open-sided, concrete-floored *sak-sak* hut on the water's edge of a generally placid ocean, was called the "*haus win*" and provided outdoor seating and an ocean viewing area near the Sergeant's Mess, lounge, and bar. (The beach front location is pictured in the opening gallery.) Some considered this venue basic, but the Nasho Six found it a comfortable and homely outdoor living space especially as most had come from standard indoor lifestyle of 1960s rural or suburban, three-bedroom homes. Alongside the NCO Mess on the beachfront was the Officers' Mess and this segregation or hierarchical separation was normal in the Army. Relationships were friendly and several

13. John relaxing in his donga, 1966.

14. The Sgts Mess housing "*sak-sak*" row; each door led to two rooms. 1966.

officers, including a Major and the Army doctor, became mates in the 2PIR AFL team. Visits between messes was rare. Euchre and 500 were extremely popular evening card games as they did not require too much thought and were comfortably accompanied by raucous conversation and a South Pacific Lager or two, known to all as "SP" or "Sepik Piss". Perhaps the only irritant was Max's penchant for always wanting the controlling bid, irrespective of the cards in his hand. "Ten no trumps" was his favourite and most annoying call. The others reckoned this matched his hungry approach to shots for goal on the football and basketball arena. Cards were a popular pastime enjoyed, to varying degrees, by all.

Being twenty years old and having already left home to study and teach, the distance from home was not a problem except for those with fiancés and romantic attachments. Communication with Australia was prohibitively expensive and even if a call could be made the person at the other end was either faint or lost in the crackle. Letters from home and an occasional package of goodies were regarded as a bonus. Bob and Margy solved the problem by resorting to the up–to-date technology of the day, the cassette player. They recorded a short chat about recent events and perhaps some private whispering and then posted it off. When Bob's package arrived in the mail, he scooted off to his donga, shut the door and shutters and lay back on his bed attentively listening to Margy's sweet voice, hence his nickname, "Sheets". Others also acquired a nickname. John became "Pants" because just as he arrived, a Sydney newspaper ran a story about a John Sweeney who was arrested for stealing underwear from the clothesline at a Nurses Hostel.

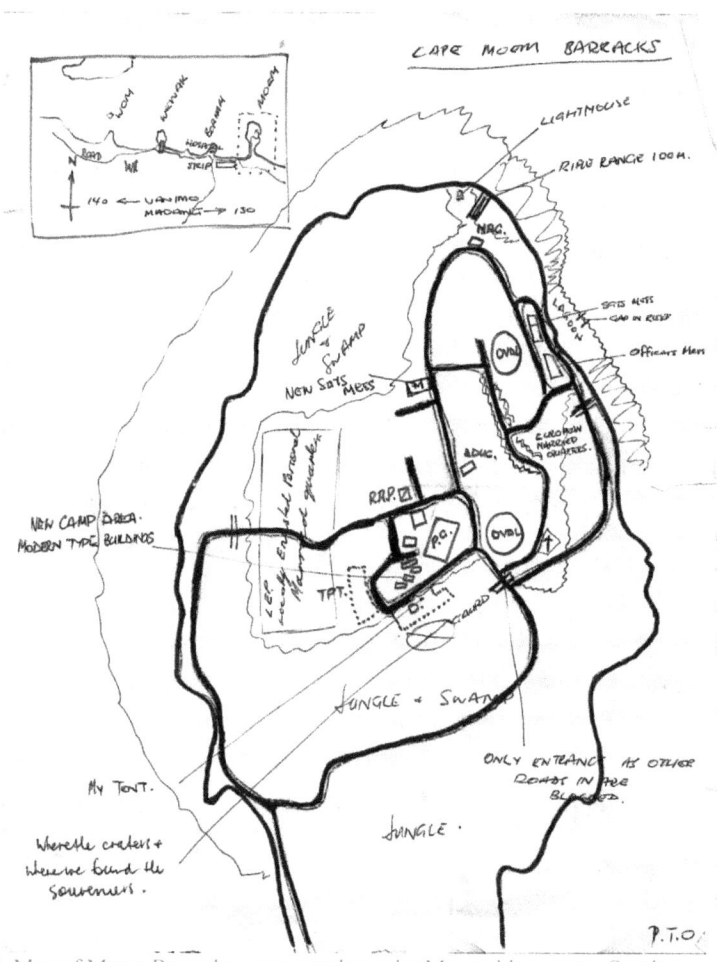

15. Map of Moem Barracks camp sent home by Max to his parents, October 1966.

He was also known inappropriately as the "Bishop's son" because his Uncle Pascal Sweeney was the Bishop at the Catholic Mission at Vanimo. Rick became "Larry" after an unfortunate encounter with the barber that resulted in a short, back and side and mop on top, á la Larry of the Three Stooges. Peter became "Black Pete" due to his deep suntanned body from surfing days back home in Newcastle. Laurie became "Fingers" because he would "do" his finger trying to take speccy marks in Aussie Rules games. Max was the only one not to acquire a nickname as his family name Quanchi was already strange enough.

Bob also received packages from Margy's Mum, and these were keenly looked forward to because Bob always shared the fruit cake and Anzac biscuits that Queenie sent up. The package always included a few back issues of the Wagin Argus and Arthur, Dumbleyung and Lake Grace Express, the local paper from around Kukerin. This allowed Bob to keep up with the cricket and footy scores, local political rumours, and wheat prices. Mail-order, vinyl LP records were popular and enjoyed almost daily.

Rick recalls he stretched himself beyond Peter, Paul, and Mary into more raunchy music such as Nancy Sinatra's "These Boots are made for Walking". It was not exactly head-banging stuff but rather cool in the 1960s.

Home seemed an awfully long way away, and Rick only learned of the death of his grandfather Leif, a WW1 veteran, through a letter from his Dad some weeks after the passing.

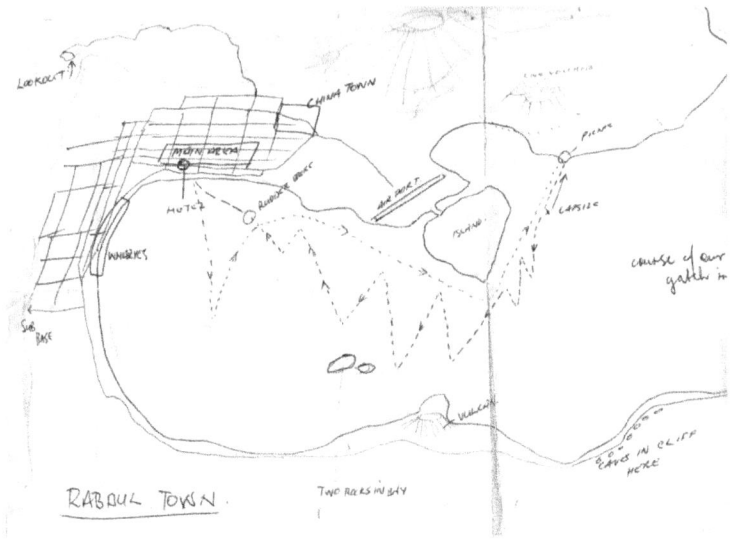

16. Map sent home by Max showing the route on a Yachting adventure during a Christmas holiday visit to Rabaul with Pete in 1966.

17. Front row of Sgts sleeping quarters, taken from the *haus win*, 1966.

Letters from home were prized and read several times in private in the donga or while catching the breeze in the *haus win*. Parents, girlfriends, or a fiancé were the most common recipients, but everyone corresponded with people they probably would not have written to back home as writing letters was a good time-filler. Re-reading letters also passed the time while laying prone with ceiling fans aimed down at the Castellani's paint which was used on the skin to cure the crutch rot some had contracted.

Not far off the coast of Moem Point was the small island of Muschu, which was idyllic although we did not realise it had been a Japanese military stronghold in WWII. Occasionally the Army launch would take a small group out for the day. The rugged landscape was broken with streams of pure water that made their way to the ocean. Rick has photographs of himself sitting under a small waterfall section of a stream perhaps two metres wide, washing his hairy armpits in tropical pleasure.

As evidence of the Army's unpreparedness and indecision about the status of the education program, and the arrival of large numbers of Nasho Chalkies in TPNG, it was not until January 1967 that the Nasho Six were issued with a PIR uniform with its distinctive Green Beret, badges, and red lanyard to denote the Infantry. This meant the Chalkies had collected an assortment of lanyards – white for Artillery, yellow for Armoured Corps, scarlet for Ordnance, blue for Education and finally red for Infantry (2PIR).

A regular adventure at Wewak was a "swan" provided when the Army's Caribou came up with supplies from Port Moresby and was heading to Vanimo or into the mountains to supply a platoon on patrol.

18. Tony Hedland (a Chalkie in the second cohort) wedding party, 1967.

19. Rick heading from his donga to the communal showers. Haus-win in the background, 1966.

This was called a "swan", in Army parlance, because it was official duty but really an excuse for a free ride. Befriending the Caribou pilots became de rigour. The Caribou was a magnificent short take-off and landing transport plane designed to carry a full platoon and gear. It was in wide use in Vietnam. Max organized a swan one day for himself and Bob in a Caribou up to Amanab station in the mountains quite close to the Indonesian border. This was a great trip with amazing coastal and then mountain scenery and the usual hair-raising landing on a noticeably short, rough, uphill, grass landing strip carved out of the jungle. Laurie was on patrol in Amanab and seemed quite casual about his mates' visit until they produced a large bunch of letters from his fiancé back in Perth. The best "swan" was to go on the Army payroll run up to Vanimo. This required an Officer along with two supporting Sergeants to guard a locked briefcase full of money. Once the pay was distributed the afternoon was free to go water-skiing behind a ubiquitous flat-bottomed runabout with a 40HP Johnson. Bob, for example, took some lessons from Max and was soon shooting over the glassy waters of Vanimo Bay. Max had already taught the CO at Vanimo how to ski, so skiing had become a compulsory part of Vanimo life. Bob had now learnt to stand up on a surfboard and to ski, all in a few months.

Another transport revolution occurred when Bob purchased Staff Sergeant Bob Wriggley's 50cc Honda. "Wriggles" had purchased a more powerful set of wheels, a 250cc twin cylinder Honda. With a bottle of Bacardi and a bundle of cash to settle the deal, Bob now had his own wheels. This inspired Max and John to purchase a more modest 30cc Yamaha Moped for $132 which could be pedalled to start the motor or to gain extra power when going up hills.

There remains an unconfirmed rumour that a Nasho had done a naked night-time moped trip around the camp roads. Surfing afternoons and trips to town no longer required a cramped trip in the red Renault Rick had shipped up from Australia. Max sold his Moped after taking two spills in the gravel on the road to town. Bob sold his Honda to a Warrant Officer Peter Mamare, a footy and basketball mate. Bob claims he took $20 off the price so that Peter could get the otherwise unlicensed motorbike licensed in town.

A less pleasant experience at Moem was malaria prevention. The 44-gallon oil drums lit at night by the Japanese to combat mosquitoes along their defensive perimeter in 1942-1945 were still in place in 1966. 2PIR tackled it more scientifically with a daily dose of paludrine for everyone, squads of soldiers each day cutting grass to reduce the breeding grounds and a weekly DDT smoke bomber going around the camp blasting a chemical spray (supposedly non-toxic) into rooms and bedrooms. Bob recalls the nightly trauma of waking to hear a chainsaw sound and billowing smoke as the DDT smoke-bomber did his rounds of the Sgts Mess sleeping quarters. The DDT squad were of course supposed to check each quarter to make sure they were not occupied, clearly a task they took on lightly. Eventually a regulation was introduced making it compulsory to wear long sleeves and long pants after 6.30pm.

Bob suffered three bouts of malaria, starting with the usual chills and shakes followed by headaches, vomiting and diarrhoea and Max was hospitalized with one nasty attack after being found exhausted and asleep on the side of the road. He was rushed off to the public hospital at Boram which gave the rest of the gang an opportunity to visit the hospital and chat up the Australian nurses who were otherwise supposed to be off-limits. Everyone was puzzled why the paludrine tablets, smoke-bomber DDT program and clothing regulations did not have more impact.

Short haircuts were mandatory and practical in the tropical heat, so Max involuntarily became the barber for the Nasho Six, and a few other Sergeants, including on one occasion, the RSM. Max also took on a private tutoring role after work for an Officer's young children to help keep them up to Australian standards.

For Christmas in 1966, the Sergeants and Officers joined forces and went to the ORs Mess and in an Army tradition, served the soldiers their Christmas dinner of fish, vegetables, pudding, and for just this occasion, a stubbie of beer. Then the Officers and Sergeants headed back and shared their joint Christmas nosh-up, and what a feast it was with all the trimmings and top quality, bottomless wines. After a siesta in the afternoon, the Officers and Sergeants reunited for a soiree with drinks and finger food in the Officers Mess. This was a rare formal get together of NCOs and officers at a social level.

Max and Pete took a short Christmas break at the end of 1966 to visit Rabaul and explored Japanese tunnels from WWII, clambered about wrecked tanks, barges and gun emplacements, scaled a volcano (dormant) and in a foolhardy adventure went sailing with a new-found mate down the harbour to visit Matupi, the live volcano at the entrance to Rabaul harbour. This was in a small single-mast yacht which could just take three adult men. The trip out the harbour and around to the base of the volcano was uneventful, except that the sulphur was overwhelming, and the water extremely hot as gases were still escaping from the vent in the ocean floor. On the way home the intrepid sailors capsized the yacht and the wind forced them back to whence they came. A second try meant tacking back and forth out into the centre of the harbour and then – horrors - the rudder broke. After drifting helplessly for half an hour, a passing motorboat towed the yacht and the three embarrassed and sunburnt tourists back to the Yacht Club. The trip to Rabaul also included the memorable and moving visit to Bitapaka War Cemetery, tended carefully by the Australian War Graves Commission. The cemetery contains the headstones of Australians killed in WWI and WWII, as well as a memorial to the AEI Submarine that disappeared off the Duke of York Islands at the start of WWI. The wreck resting on the sea floor was finally found by a marine salvage operation and search team in January 2018. The Bitapaka cemetery includes the graves and a commemorative wall in honour of the soldiers who died in the short campaign to capture an important radio station on the Gazelle Peninsula from the Germans at the outbreak of World War I. This mostly forgotten campaign has finally been honoured. The Papua New Guineans who fought for the Germans in WWI and for the Japanese in WWII have not yet received recognition.

An occasion for mingling with the local Wewak population was provided by the start of a four-team Wewak Australian Rules competition, with one Army team, and teams from town, the Catholic Mission and Brandi High School. Rick, Laurie, Bob and Max were stalwarts for the Army team, but Pete also had a brief foray into what was a strange code for an NSW boy. Papua New Guinean players excelled as the flair and opportunism and variety of skills in Aussie Rules appealed to their approach to sport. Sporting events at Moem Barracks also included an occasional challenge match against a team from town, or inter-service cricket and rugby matches when naval ships made a rare port of call. With an Army football team in the town competition, plus basketball, volleyball, softball, and married team competitions, that the initial cohort of Nashos initiated, this created a significant Army-Town relationship enjoyed by later Nashos at Moem, and PIR generally.

A common pastime was photography, and the group amassed a huge collection of Kodak, Agfa or Ilford transparencies, or colour slides, although some black and white prints were also taken. The best colour was produced by Kodak. Max had purchased his "Kodak Instamatic 100" for $13.75, a real bargain he told his parents, while at Manly doing his Artillery training. The rolls of film were posted away to Kodak in Sydney in special posting packages provided on purchase. In most cases these were not seen until returning to Australia.

Today, this collection of several thousand images constitutes a remarkable archive of Australian involvement in the TPNG in the 1960s, and of what went on at Moem Barracks in those years. A plan is underway to digitise these images and return them to Moem Barracks, an idea started when Peter went back to Moem in 2017 on a P&O cruise around PNG. It was pointed out to Peter that soldiers of the PIR from that time never saw themselves in images like these and that today's servicemen would be excited to have the chance to look back for old mates still serving or discharged and sadly, for deceased comrades from the early days of 2PIR.

WWII relics were not immediately visible inside the Camp, but there were rumours of extensive caves and gun positions on the nearby ridges behind Wewak airport, hospital and town. 2PIR Moem Barracks was built on a former Japanese base. Only recently the Wewak Six discovered that late in the war, Wewak had been Japan's major naval and air base in the New Guinea campaigns, with hundreds of aircraft and supporting corps around Moem. In 1944-45, Wewak was left 'contained' under MacArthur's policy of 'island-hopping' around heavily fortified Japanese bases and moving on quickly to recapture the Philippines, from where he had been embarrassingly expelled by the Japanese at the outset of the war.

The Japanese base at Moem Point was 'contained' for the duration of the war and was not retaken until the Japanese surrendered in New Guinea a few days after the surrender in Japan in August 1945. A highlight occurred when the Nasho Six wandered ten metres behind D Company's lines into the fringing jungle that had once been the landward perimeter of the Japanese defences at Moem Point. Amid the trenches and bomb craters were 44-gallon drums still full of oil, once used to create smoke as a malaria prevention. When using a long stick to poke around in a drum everyone jumped when it appeared a head was being pulled out of the oil – it was a perfectly preserved Japanese gas mask. Canteens and helmets scarred with bullet holes and the other detritus of war lay all about and were so prolific and ordinary that no one bothered to collect and bring home any as souvenirs.

The Wewak Six had completed their basic teacher training prior to Nasho so there was no urgency about getting further qualifications. However, Rick and Bob decided they could not waste two years swanning around in New Guinea. Bob enrolled for the WA Teachers Higher Certificate by correspondence at the Education Centre in Subiaco. So, after demolishing a bottle of tomato sauce at tea-time, and listening to Margy's tapes, Bob would put on a few LPs and hit the books. Rick recalls sitting for one his University Philosophy examinations at Moem with one of the Education Corps officers supervising. This took place in Rick's donga, and the Lieutenant dozed off through the whole examination. Bob and Rick later convinced the Camp CO to send them home to Australia early so they could sit the final exams. Meanwhile the others stayed on to play cards, darts and watch movies in the *haus win*.

20. Peter's PIR belt (with PIR insignia buckle), PIR beret (faded) and four Service medals.

CHAPTER SIX

MATTERS EDUCATIONAL

There were roughly one thousand Papua New Guineans, both privates, NCOs and Officers at Moem Barracks, and at some stage all soldiers were expected to do "Education". The daily lessons and regular testing to meet certificate requirements was a revolutionary idea with little advance preparation but the heavy work was taken up enthusiastically by the Chalkie Sergeants while the Officers handled the paperwork, conducted examinations, and flew up to test the Infantry Company posted on rotation to Vanimo. There been a half-hearted attempt in Port Moresby to orientate the newly arrived Nasho Chalkie Sergeants but when they arrived at Moem they really had no idea of appropriate Army protocols and traditions and it seemed nobody at Moem was ready for this large-scale invasion of youthful Australian expertise. There was not much in the way of facilities and hardly any resources. The Education unit consisted of a Captain and two Lieutenants. The Nasho Sergeants were each immediately allocated to infantry or administration companies as an Education specialist.

The purpose of this rapidly expanded Education project was to advance the battle-ready status of the Army that Australia had started to build in TPNG as it approached self-government. The aim was to teach newly recruited village boys how to speak and read in English, with some basic Arithmetic, Civics and Social Studies. The target was to reach PCOE standard, or Proficiency Certificate in Oral English. Teaching was mostly at the conversational English level as few older soldiers or new recruits could speak, read, or write in English. All Army manuals, commands and orders were given in English so for PIR to become a national, battle-ready and unifying force in the new nation, a rapid language expansion program for soldiers had to be put in place. As the Nasho Chalkies would do the classroom teaching, the initial strategy was for a Sergeant instructor to be embedded in each of the four rifle companies and the two support companies, with one Sergeant retained at the Education Centre to help with advanced courses and records. The Education Centre in 1966 was a low *sak-sak* building in the middle of the base with an office at the front and a small classroom at the rear. There was additional teaching space alongside in a large Army marquee. Within a few days Laurie was posted as B Company's Education Specialist Instructor as one infantry Company was always rostered on rotation at the Vanimo base. Almost immediately Peter also took off in an Army Cessna to join his designated infantry Company, A Coy, which was then out on patrol at Green River near the West New Guinea/Indonesian border. A week later he returned to Wewak in a Caribou, the first of many flights. There Peter met Max, Bob, Rick and John. It was several months before Laurie returned from Vanimo and joined the group back at Moem.

21. Education Centre, May 1966. Office to the front (left), teaching space at rear (right).

Max was sent to teach in a tent in the jungle on the edge of the Moem Barracks where D Company was housed while waiting for their new barracks to be built. Bob taught in a small tent near Admin Company where he waited for soldiers to come and present their homework and then be given the next day's homework. Attendance for Admin Company was voluntary and had to be done in the soldier's free time. This system failed. Soon it was then decided to bring all Education Sergeants back to the Education Centre and run courses on a monthly rotation allocated by each Company CO, with compulsory attendance. The Education team settled in instructing ORs in basic conversational English and Social Studies. When Max was seconded as Regimental Sports Officer, charged with starting up sporting competitions and getting sporting facilities in place, and with one Nasho posted at Vanimo, and one usually off on patrol, it meant a reduced team had to handle all the teaching.

The age of the soldiers varied from 17 to 40 years, recruited from districts across TPNG. Some were raw recruits straight out of boot camp at the Goldie River Training Barracks near Port Moresby, and some students were wizened non-commissioned officers with a decade or more of Army service. At home in their villages some had attended a local primary school usually run by Missions, but few had secondary schooling. English was often the second, third or fourth language of the new PIR recruits. Teaching therefore was a difficult and slow process.

Progress was sequential through a series of certificates that indicated familiarity initially with conversational English language – words, phrases and sentences, leading on to conventional secondary level studies in written English and reading. The structure was simple;

IOE	Intermediate Oral English
PCOE	Proficiency Certificate in Oral English
IACE	Intermediate Army Certificate of Education
SACE	Senior Army Certificate of Education.

Education for children throughout the TPNG was erratically available in the 1950s and 1960s and was provided, where it could be accessed, by both the Government and Churches. Local teachers often had no more than Primary education themselves supplemented by, in many instances, teacher training programs of less than a year.

Pre-testing to establish reading and writing levels of competency, a conventional procedure back in Australia, was set aside at Moem. Getting the soldiers up to a level of basic conversational English, with some broader enhancement in geography, history and social studies was a noble objective, but required a degree of patience and enthusiasm. The Army Education Corps had not provided for, and did not seem to have detailed, practical strategies for this national development project. This education component of Army life was of course only a small part of the soldier's daily routine of marching, patrolling, drills, exercises, weapon training, sport, ground maintenance, and personal cleanliness. Being literate was important but secondary to being battle-ready.

The Wewak Chalkies were not trained in Teaching English as a Second Language. Everyone just battled along making it up on a day-to-day basis. The daily schedule involved tests and exams for the more advanced students, dreaming up new worksheets for others, and managing the intricacies of the temperamental gestetner copying machine. When Infantry companies went on patrol their Education Sergeants went along or just had a slack period back at camp until the company came back to base.

Teaching was based on rote learning and constant repetition. A class of fifty minutes with thirty soldiers was hot and sweaty work especially in the canvas tents used before classes were centralized at the new Education Centre building. The floor of the tent was bare earth and the desks and chairs the only furniture. Classes started at 8.30am and finished at 4.30pm with a 90-minute lunch break. The teacher introduced words and phrases and the soldiers mimicked the sounds parrot fashion. A typical English language class started with the instructor identifying an object, for example, a pencil, saying "pencil" and then asking the soldiers to repeat the word as many times as it took until the instructor was satisfied. Then it was on to the next word. The more advanced certificate courses in English proficiency involved basic writing and reading. The Nasho Six ploughed on.

Bob remembers starting a class with the injunction "luk im noa" (look at this, in *Tok pisin*, despite all lessons supposedly being in English) or "wan em" (what is this?) Then on to the next gimmick – a comb, piece of fruit, a belt, a book – or whatever inspirational object and word could be conjured up for a group sweltering in a humid, hot *sak-sak* or tent classroom. Tattered, lined exercise books were then used by the soldiers to record the new word or phrase. The success of this teaching had to be tested by one of the Education Corps officers. Bob recalls being up at Vanimo Base when a group of soldiers were due to be tested for their IOE, leading to a promotion for some from Lance-Corporal to Corporal. The Officer from Moem Barracks sent up for the testing arrived by commercial flight for a three or four day "swan" to conduct the afternoon's testing. One test went like this – the officer asks a Chimbu from Mt Hagen, "What is this?" while holding up a comb. This soldier had been in the Catering Corps for eight years. The soldier replied "comb". Bob was smirking at his brilliant success when the officer then asked "What am I doing?" while pretending to comb his hair, the soldier confidently and quickly replied "*upela strait em gras*" (meaning, you are combing your hair). A second attempt by the officer led to the answer "*upela strait em gras. Em long on top moa moa yet*" (You are combing the exceptionally long hair on top of your head). After being informed the test had to be conducted solely in English, the soldier gave an immaculate salute and a "Yes Sir", turned and marched out. The Officer laughed and turned to Bob and said the soldier had passed and would be "Corporal before you know it".

This soldier did move up to Corporal but on Bob's advice stayed on in the IOE class for a few extra months. The camp CO at Moem later came up with the idea of voluntary Saturday morning lectures on topics of world interest or current affairs, decided by the CO and delivered by the Education Corps Sergeants. These sessions were not popular and were gradually abandoned. Max still has the printed AACE Current Affairs lecture notes on Communism, the Vietnam War, the Middle East, and World Affairs, couched in a language of support for Western democracy. (See Appendix E) Another innovation was the introduction of "Library Nights" to allow soldiers to come and read books and write letters. Max did the first night of this new duty, and no-one turned up until he rang the infantry companies and about twenty soldiers showed up briefly. This experiment dragged on desultorily until it was abandoned.

In January 1967, Max reported home to his parents that everyone had "really got stuck into Education now ... half the Company in the morning and half in the afternoon ... so it means big classes ... 61 in the morning and 50 in the afternoon at about Grade 3-4 Standard English ... squashed into one Army marquee. They are as hot as the proverbial". The roster involved teaching a group for five weeks and then changing groups.

The building program at Moem Barracks was proceeding throughout 1967 and eventually, late in the year, Education moved into a brand-new double-storied Centre. This was palatial after teaching in the previous Education *haus win* and in tents out in the infantry companies.

There were some teaching aids provided by the Army. The most valuable was a set of simple primers published by the Australian Commonwealth Department of Education, meant for use by European migrants coming to Australia after WW11. The content was presented in comic-book fashion and focused on Australian town and bush life, but the PIR soldiers enjoyed reading these books once they had advanced to PCOE level. The soldiers copied everything into their own dusty tattered exercise books. Another set of readers were designed and produced in TPNG for local schools. Another called Nuis, (news) in newsletter format, presented stories about New Guinea people, animals, events, and sites and included photographs. (Max later used these photographs as part of his PhD on early black and white photography in colonial New Guinea.) The classroom uses of these materials followed the familiar pattern – Sergeant reads a sentence, and a soldier or soldiers reiterate the sentence. Rick remembers the English support material as being basic and often culturally unsuitable. For a bunch of young inexperienced teachers thrown into this situation with minimal training, Rick thinks they did OK, surviving without basic educational instruction materials and surprised regularly to see progress in the students. When Rick returned to TPNG as a civilian Psychologist, he learned that the intelligence tests the Army had used were notoriously unreliable in this type of cultural setting.

Some soldiers advanced rapidly, like "Leonard" (not his real name) from Bougainville. In his first PCOE class the copperplate writing in his exercise book stood out, so Leonard was asked to read a page from Nuis. He read it in perfect English. After the class, Bob asked Leonard about his writing and reading, and it turned out he had done five years in a Mission school on Bougainville. This fact had not been recorded in his enlistment papers. He was immediately advanced to the next course and started doing the IACE. By the time, the Nasho Six departed

TPNG, Leonard was a Corporal and about to sit his exams for the next level, the SACE. Two years later he was selected for Officer Training at Portsea Officers School in Australia. This quietly spoken young man had demonstrated exactly what the Nasho Chalkie education scheme was all about – opening doors for personal advancement and the development of a nation in the making.

The ICAE was roughly equivalent to Year 10 secondary level in Australia. This was a huge leap for soldiers coming from village schools, and even more so for those advancing to SACE which was set at the Australian matriculation or Year 12 level. At this level soldiers were confronted with Civics Education, Grammar, and essay writing skills. Typically, this involved forty minutes drafting an essay followed by ten minutes reading the essay of the soldier alongside. This was confronting for soldiers, as although PNG is reputedly an egalitarian society, this level of familiarity and personal exposure was difficult for most soldiers to accept. This approach widely used back in Australian classrooms had to be tailored carefully to cater for soldiers' reluctance to speak out in front of strangers or to share their work with others.

Generally, the pattern was get up in the morning, change into heavily starched uniform shorts and shirts, breakfast and off to the respective Company or later the Education Centre, to teach whatever was the order of the day – usually conversational English. Everyone had their own favourite stories shared at the end of the day in the Sergeants Mess over a cold beer.

At the end of 1967, replacement Education Sergeants started arriving but there was no formal hand-over or a period of transitional training to prepare the new Chalkie instructors for what

EDITORIAL

Time keeps on moving. Many things do not change but we can always be sure that time will go on - it never stands still. A wise man once said, " Time and tide wait for no man." This means that of all things that man may one day control or be able to change or slow down, the time of day or year and the movement of the sea in tides will not be one of these things.

As time passes we are drawing near to the time of the year that many people find unpleasant - the 30th of June, the end of the financial year. This is the time when every person must make an account of the money he has received and pay his share of running the government. This is also the time when the government begins to work out how it will spend the money it has received.

As Papua - New Guinea advances towards independence and responsible government, its people must become more responsible. This is why all Papuans and New Guineans have to pay a share of their wages towards the cost of government. We call this way the government has of raising money to do its job INCOME TAX.

22. Front cover of the Newsletter Max produced in his role as Meom Barracks Sports Officer. Printed on the Education Centre gestetner duplicating machine.

they would face. It was just a "Hi guys" and "Get on with it" approach. It seemed to the team at Wewak that this was typical of the whole Chalkie and educational expansion scheme. It was agreed during discussions with the second round of Chalkies, that the Nasho education scheme was a good idea but that the Army could have done a better job preparing, monitoring, and applying the expertise available to the task of expanding educational provisions for soldiers in the PIR. The new guys just dug in and took over.

By mid-1967 the Army had also built a school for Army children with four civilian teachers at Moem Barracks. This meant the children of Officers and Sergeants and married ORs no longer had to travel into Wewak for schooling. Max joked to his parents that, "we just about have to start a Union here". The school operated quite independently of the Army's Education Corps activities.

On occasions, classes included Australian officers as there was an Army requirement that Second Lieutenants pass the Army Education Certificate Class 1 as a pathway to becoming First Lieutenants. One of Rick's roles was to take an English class, roughly at Australian Year 12 level. Rick remembers introducing this group to the literary heritage of Ernest Hemingway. They were younger officers and quite receptive.

There had been rumours throughout the posting to 2PIR about how long the Chalkie posting would last. Initially a year was mentioned. Then extended to 15 months and then indefinite. Talk of leaving was revived in September 1967 when it was announced that eight replacement Nasho Chalkies would arrive. Finally, when a new Education Corps Commanding Officer, a Lt Colonel, was posted to Port Moresby he announced the departure would be in December. The indecision over departure was compounded by a lack of clarity from the various State Education Departments about discharge and returning to teaching. As late as October the Victorian Education Department was still talking of a five-week refresher course for Nashos. (It never took place.) A further scare took place when it was announced by Army Command in Port Moresby that all Nashos had to serve out their accrued leave at Command headquarters in Port Moresby before returning to Australia, thereby forgoing their accrued leave pay. Luckily, the Adjutant at Moem thought this was a silly idea and sent the Wewak Six back home, with the task of reporting to each State Command HQ just prior to discharge date.

The six Nasho Sergeants finished their teaching duties, packed their bags and left TPNG and apart from one or two successful soldiers whose names popped up now and then in the news when they had entered politics, the Nasho Six never found out if their education efforts for two years with 2PIR had been worthwhile or productive. The break with 2PIR and TPNG was therefore sudden and complete. Regrettably there were few continuing links with individual Australian or Papua New Guinean soldiers who had shared many of the incidents related in these stories.

CHAPTER SEVEN

MATTERS MILITARY

The 2nd Battalion of the Pacific Islands Regiment (2PIR) was partnered by 1PIR, the Battalion stationed at Port Moresby, the capital of TPNG. In 1966, when the Nasho six arrived, the island of New Guinea was divided into three parts. The western half had been a Dutch East Indies colony. By defeating the Dutch in 1949 in a war of independence, Indonesia had been united as new nation and in 1961 invaded the remaining former Dutch territory. It gained international approval in 1963 to stay on until a plebiscite would be held in 1969. The north-eastern region, a United Nations Trusteeship administered by Australia, was formerly a German Colony, and a south-eastern region, formerly a British Colony, was a territory (or colony) of Australia. After WWII, the two eastern entities were administered as one Territory by Australia and called TPNG. The Pacific Islands Regiment had grown out of the Papuan Infantry Battalion (See, Hank Nelson, "As bilong soldia: The raising of the Papuan Infantry battalion in 1940", *Yagl-Ambu*, Vol 7, 1, 1980, pp.20-27) raised during World War II and in 1966 had bases and training camps at Vanimo, Wewak, Lae, Mt Hagen, Port Moresby and Goldie River. The PIR was in a development phase and regarded as part of the Australian Armed Forces, in preparation for becoming the Army of the new nation that would one day emerge.

The international border between TPNG and the western half of the island of New Guinea, renamed "Irian Jaya" by Indonesia, was a line on survey maps but with large blank areas where aerial mapping had been obscured by cloud. Platoons from 2PIR at Vanimo and Wewak regularly patrolled along the border, as well as completing mapping and checking 'secret' refugee camps and carrying out surveillance of the Indonesian Army patrols doing the same thing on the other side of the unmarked border. The Vanimo camp was situated strategically close to Hollandia/Sukarnapura, a mere 40 kilometres away. An Army Caribou (short take-off and landing transport plane) could airlift a platoon from Vanimo to the border in a matter of minutes. Although Indonesia was an ally of the USA, it was alleged to be susceptible to communist influences, a Cold War scenario recently involving nearby Malaya, Indonesia and Borneo and currently being fought on the ground in Vietnam. An understanding of global politics was beyond the Nasho Six at Moem, and they remained ignorant of the Indonesian-Papuan tragedy unfolding across the border. The existence of West Papuan refugee camps on the TPNG side of the border was not discussed in the Sergeants Mess or well-known widely even though it was later learnt that there had been sizeable camps at, for example, Morehead in the Daru district and at Pagei just south of Vanimo. The Nasho Six regarded Vanimo, not as a possible front-line base in a border conflict, but as a tropical beachside resort.

In the 1960s, the Cold War, China's resurgence, recent wars in Korea, Borneo and Malaya, fear of Communist expansion into

Indonesia and escalating conflict in Vietnam were central to military thinking about PNG's preparedness as a nation. On the rare occasions when geopolitics were discussed in the Sergeant's Mess or *haus win*, that rhetoric was obsessively militaristic, and anti-Communist.

In 1967, a new Regimental Sergeant-Major (the "RSM") was appointed at Moem Barracks. The RSM, for ordinary soldiers, was the immediate face of the Army and equal in status to the Majors, Captains and Lieutenants who stood in the army hierarchy under the Battalion Commanding Officer, a Lt Colonel. While below Officer Rank, as the leading NCO and direct link to the foot-soldiers or ORs, the RSM was respected, acknowledged even by Officers, and indeed feared by all. The RSM was the Commanding Officer's right-hand man and thoroughly a soldier's soldier, who by demeanour, military record and experience was really the key factor in a regiment's standing in Army terms. Into this hierarchical military club marched the new RSM, Daryl Howells. He was regular Australian Army, but little known, young, and not so obviously military in manner and attitude. To the six Chalkie Sergeants he was simply "Daryl" or DH. Prior to his promotion he had enjoyed the unusual Sergeants Mess scenario of having the company of young, sporty, university educated young men, and he had been a companion to the new Nasho Sergeants in the Mess, joining in games of darts and organizing trips in his rather impressive car at the time, a Toyota Corona, out to Cape Wom, west of Wewak where the Japanese surrender in New Guinea had been signed in September 1945 and on another occasion to Brandi River reservoir, which supplied the base and Wewak town with water. The new RSM shared many urbane and intellectual pursuits and often invited his current, favourite Nasho Sergeant over to his house, a little down the beach and separate from the Mess, for dinner. He once dragged Rick and Max off to Church. Once he became RSM the relationship changed. This was the military way.

The rather un-military behaviour of Nasho Sergeants attracted some criticism, often in the form of a barbed comment, or the RSM's favourite, "Not impressed Sergeant, lift your game". The usual outcome was being put on roster as Duty Sergeant for a day which involved early morning and late afternoon drill parade when soldiers caught for one or other infringement were marched back and forward by a Duty Sergeant around the parade ground. To the Nasho Sergeants, the worst penalty was weekend Orderly Duty Sergeant which meant you lost your precious free time for social and sporting pursuits.

Army life for the locally enlisted personnel was exciting and an introduction to the wider world, but also involved separation from wontoks and their own communities. The Army did its best to ameliorate the loneliness and paid attention to cultural matters. This was demonstrated when a Corporal died without any apparent external or internal injuries. Max wrote home to his parents about this incident saying, "He was a Chimbu, one of the most progressive and stick-together tribes in the country. So, everyone was a little anxious to avoid trouble on the camp as pay-backs are still prevalent. However, there was none of that, but many soldiers were upset as he was very popular and had lots of one-talks … the Chimbu soldiers wanted him buried in "Chimbu-land". So, this morning his body was brought from the hospital to the Church and a Catholic Mass and ceremony were held, and then the coffin was taken to Wewak airport where the body was piped into the plane. It was a very solemn and impressive ceremony with the 2PIR pipers playing a funeral dirge."

An Army obsession with fitness meant regular testing of fitness for ORs and NCOs. The Nashos had confronted the packmarch back in basic training, so the 4.8km run scheduled for all NCOs was considered a breeze. Around 4am a convey of trucks took everyone down the road towards Wewak town and after a roll call the RSM ordered everyone back to Barracks, either running, jogging or walking within the allowed forty minutes. Fail and it would be repeated each day until a pass was achieved. The SLR and full pack added a little extra strain when everyone set off enthusiastically under the watchful eye of the RSM. There was no prize for being first back through the camp gates, but everyone checked their watches to make sure they complied with the set time allocated. A few of the older regular Army NCOs struggled a bit, panting and often walking but the Nashos set an exhilarating example. While regarded as quite a funny experience at the time, Bob now recalls it nearly killed him, suggesting he was not as fit as he thought. Stragglers were picked up by the trucks following along behind. Pleased with this level of fitness the RSM then announced a compulsory ten mile (16km) "forced march" for all NCOs. The start time was 3am. After the roll call, the contingent marched back towards Moem Point. Stragglers soon fell behind and were collected by the trucks. After two hours steady marching the gates of the camp appeared in the early morning light. The Chalkies had all passed and the RSM ticked off their names. Breakfast back at the Mess was truly enjoyed by all that morning.

Next on the RSM's battle-preparedness agenda was arms training, so in preparation the Education Sergeants organized a training session down at the firing range carved out of the jungle on Moem Point. Bob had already fired the Owen gun, the Browning automatic pistol, and the new Swedish issue SLR during his Cadet days, and Rick and Max had been handy rabbit shooters with a .22 rifle. For the others, any sort of weapon was a new experience. The rifle range ran a few hundred metres down a clearing in the jungle to a five metre high, sand-bagged earthwork that backed on to the beach. This had been the new RSM's idea, and he had created this new range especially for 2PIR's use. Anything that went over the top of the earth wall ended up well out to sea, potentially endangering and certainly scaring locals passing along the coast in their canoes. A red flag supposedly warned them about live firing at the range. The firing area was sand-bagged and supposedly under strict protocols.

Of course, the Nasho Six did Rambo impersonations and blasted away at a set of standard Army-issue targets. The targets suffered little damage from these efforts and plumes of water out to sea indicated that much of the fire went well out to sea above the retaining wall. This was particularly obvious when trying to master the Infantry's most powerful weapon, the M60 machine gun. It was an American general-purpose machine gun using 7.62mm cartridges from a disintegrating belt and had been introduced in the Vietnam War in 1964. It could be fired as single shot or repeat. Nashos had not been able to fire the M60 during recruit training, so everyone took the opportunity to blast away. The M60 was usually fired using a tripod but could also be fired from the shoulder or hip. Hanging on grimly the Nasho Six each stepped up and had a go firing in ten to twenty-round bursts. But Bob, keeping his finger on the trigger far too long caused the belt to jam, much to the RSM's displeasure.

23. Laurie Bowman, RSM Daryl Howells and Peter Suna, in front of the Sgts Mess, 1967.

A quick repair job by the RSM and again young Bob, "let her rip". Not anticipating the kickback, Bob let loose a great long burst. The initial twenty rounds destroyed the target, but the remainder smashed into the RSMs brand new sand-bagged retaining wall or went over the top and well out to sea. The RSM was not impressed. Bob's punishment was a weekend Orderly Sergeant roster. The only casualty from all this noise and military fire power was John, who developed tinnitus, and still endures this condition.

Rick had been an Air Force Cadet at school and had used both .22 and .303 rifles. He had also done a bit of rabbit shooting on farming properties. Rick had also received very basic training in 9mm pistol instruction at Bandiana and a decision was made to have Rick supervise a group of ORs on the pistol range where cardboard figures had been set up as targets in front of the RSM's new earthen wall. Papua New Guinean soldiers were generally not tall, although this depended upon their place of origin in the country. Private Willy was an exception. Willy was a big fellow, obliging and always seeking to do his best. So, when his pistol jammed what did Willy do? He asked Sgt Rick for help. The way he did so did not conform to regulations. He turned pointing the pistol at Rick, saying, "Sergeant, pistol it is stuck". Rick's shocked but rulebook response was immediate, "Willy, turn back and face the target." Rick then thanked Willy for obeying and then spelt-out firmly the appropriate rifle range response to a jammed pistol if such an incident should occur again.

The purpose of all this military preparation was of course secret and never discussed openly in the Sergeants Mess but it soon became apparent that it was all about mobilization, Army language for having a Battalion ready to take action at short notice. If mobilization occurred the Military Police would rouse everyone, gear and weapons would be collected from the Armoury and NCOs would report to the RSM for battle orders. The response team would be trucked to the nearby Wewak aerodrome for uplifting by Army Caribou to the designated trouble spot. So, it was mostly wait, and wait, wait, wait … and more waiting until there was an order to spring into action. The enemy that PIR might be mobilized against was unclear, but in Canberra perhaps relations with Indonesia over West New Guinea were tense and war games were probably being played out on the planning table at HQ in Port Moresby. Meanwhile up at Moem Barracks, the Nasho Sergeants just shrugged and took it all in as part of typically nonsensical Army war games. The reward for all this route marching and rifle practice was that soldiers were granted a "stand-down" day, in which all normal military activity was suspended. For the Chalkies it meant a day at Brandi Beach or a day lazing about the Mess in civvies.

Readers can be assured that in 1966-67 the Nasho Six at Moem Barracks were doing their best to appear military and were definitely battle-ready and eager to rush into mobilization mode. The RSM took all this military stuff very seriously as he had served in the Malayan campaign and was careful to tick all the right boxes with military command in Port Moresby.

Although rarely mentioned at 2PIR in 1966-1967 everyone knew about the Nashos who had gone to Vietnam. Max wrote home in February 1967 that at Moem, "everyone is astir over the shelling of Australian soldiers in Vietnam". The Current Affairs talks inspired by these events and introduced by the base CO and delivered by Nasho Chalkies, were pro-democracy and anti-Communist in spirit although dressed up as Civics lessons. Meanwhile the Nasho Six continued to enjoy their occasional forays into matters military and perhaps somewhat half-heartedly saluted and marched their way through the eighteen months of their posting.

In 2001, rioting by soldiers over the PNG government's proposal to halve the size of the Army led to some buildings at Moem being burnt down. In another riot on the base in 2002, the Education Centre was burnt down, not as a deliberate targeting of Education, but merely because it was near the centre of action.

24. A framed photography Peter has today of the meeting below.

25. Peter has just woken up at Telefomin and it was a bright sunny day. Peter is in off-duty dress (no belt or beret). The local is wearing a koteka, or penis gourd and carrying his string bag or *bilum*.

CHAPTER EIGHT

ON PATROL

2PIR at Moem Barracks was in the vast Sepik region which included a long coastline and offshore islands, a coastal mountain range and the massive ranges of the central cordillera. Between the two ranges was the majestic Sepik River basin and its wide flood plain and many different language groups who claimed parts of this terrain as their ancestral lands. Moem and Vanimo were the natural take-off points for patrolling the Indonesian border and this enormous region.

Patrolling is a key facet of an Army's role and the PIR had the extra burden of patrolling terrain with large areas of the army survey maps left blank because cloud had obscured the land during aerial mapping after WWII. PIR patrols were sent to fill in these blank spots, and to carry out reconnaissance along the Indonesian border, to establish a presence in parts of the territory that were rarely visited by the government, and to carry out training exercises to prepare soldiers for battle conditions. Another purpose of these patrols, although not disclosed to Nasho Education Sergeants, was to carry out surveillance of West Papuan refugee camps popping up along the TPNG side of the border as West Papuans fled after the Indonesian take-over. Patrolling was serious military business but the Nasho Six treated it as a chance to see the country, especially the isolated, rugged interior which was largely inaccessible in those days. The Army was generally well-received by villagers and this welcome seemed authentic. However, isolation sometimes meant village people were sometimes untrusting, as they were traditionally suspicious of their neighbouring villagers.

On patrol everyone carried a full backpack of rations, cooking and sleeping equipment plus a weapon. The patrols generally followed semi-established trails but relied on guides who had local knowledge of the trails which often involved knee to thigh deep water or balancing on branches laid to keep a person above the mud. Leeches found these conditions conducive. Tok Pisin was spoken on patrol and Nashos were expected to be competent speakers. The soldiers took extra care of their Nasho instructors and each night they would quickly construct for them an above-ground, sleeping rig of poles and canvas, realizing that raw young Aussie Chalkies were unlikely to build a bed stable enough to last a night in the rain. The routes did not look too challenging on Royal Australian Survey Corps maps printed just that year, 1966, but the terrain and vegetation were straight out of Phantom comics. Villages were perched on high ridges or floated somewhere in flood plains. Many villagers had not seen Australians before.

The daily routine on patrol was to march (or wade, climb or slide in the mud) all day in single file for fifty minutes with a ten-minute breather in between. Scouts went ahead to check on the path and look for possible route diversions. Lunch was a snack. The main meal was at night when a bivouac camp was set up which involved cutting poles for hammocks and creating beds that swung a good metre above the ground. This was necessary to avoid being flooded in rainstorms and to keep "nasties" from your sleeping bag.

Max took off late in 1966 on a three-week patrol from Amanab to Green River, checking trails, and maps and showing the flag to rarely visited villages. This was a 100km patrol but ended taking four weeks (roughly about 4km per day) mostly following tracks between villages. Typically, this involved tackling the full range of topographical challenges from up and down steep ravines, crossing raging streams, wading through endless swampy plains and following narrow trails in the deep dark jungle while stepping over death adders coiled under leaves. Trying to maintain an erect stance seemed impossible on the slippery paths. A resupply at a convenient cleared area along the route meant a fresh supply of USA rations were either landed by Caribou at small local strips or just airdropped by small planes into the jungle as accurately as possible. The USA rations were terrific and were still in an experimental stage for the Vietnam War. In one incident, which Max is now embarrassed by, he swapped a tin of spam for a bow and set of arrows with a New Guinean whom the patrol met along a track. The arrows were made with thin bamboo shafts and fitted with re-useable spear tips designed for either small or large fish, small or large birds, possums, and pigs. The man was out for a day's hunting. (Max still has this bow and set of arrows on display in his home.) On one occasion the patrol was on a ridge and it was possible to look across a steep ravine to a village on the other side. It took three days to slip and slide down the slope, cross the raging river below and climb the ridge on the

26. A section of Peter's patrol to Telefomin, posing at one of the Administration buildings.

27. Villagers assembled at the Telefomin Admin Post for a meeting with the Kiap. The post had been opened in 1948. The memorial plinth is for two Kiaps and two Police killed in 1953. Thirty villagers were arrested and given a ten-year sentence. Their motive was never established.

other side. By the time the patrol reached the village all the inhabitants had fled into the bush and although the patrol waited two days camped on the outskirts, the villagers never showed up.After this patrol, in an article Max wrote for the Army Education Corp's Newsletter in 1967, he noted that "the influence of the District Officers (known as Kiaps) is becoming quite strong even in the out of the way areas ... local government has recently begun to operate in the area but it will be a long time before the people realise fully the benefits of organization and unity". The story of the kiaps, agricultural extension officers and patrolling is told in Jim Sinclair, Kiap: *Australia's patrol officers in Papua New Guinea (1994)*, August Kituai, *My Gun, My Brother: The World of the Papua New Guinea Colonial Police, 1920-1960* (1998) and a Ph.D thesis by Kim Godbold, "*Didiman*: Australian agricultural extension officers in the Territory of Papua and New Guinea, 1945–1975"(2009). See also, Graham Taylor, *A Kiap's Story: A decade in the life and work of an Australian Patrol Officer in the Kokoda, Madang, New Britain, New Ireland and Sepik Regions of Papua New Guinea 1948-1958*, (Pukpuk Publishing, or, direct from the author at < tay.29@bigpond.com >)

Peter's most memorable patrol was in early December 1966 when he flew with a platoon to Pagei Valley close to the West New Guinea, or Irian Jaya, border for a four-day reconnaissance and training patrol. Peter was responsible for the emergency medical kit, importantly including syringes and morphine. The rations were "native" meaning rice, tinned beef, and biscuits rather than USA Army packs or western diet. One hour into the patrol they crossed a raging river hand-over-hand along a rope. The soldier

28. View out the open back doors of a Caribou, 100 metres above the waves flying westward towards Vanimo. Sissano Lagoon is visible at left.

29. Pagei Administration post, school and landing strip 1966 (Photo: Trevor Freestone).

sent to take the rope across had been initially swept fifty metres downstream. The rest of the route Peter recalls was wading through swamps, deserted villages, with monsoonal rain every night. The occasional vista through a gap in the forest cover was a reminder of PNG's wildness and beauty. Bob's first patrol went along the beach east of Vanimo down to a Mission station at Leitre (in the Rawo language area of today's Sanduan Province). Supposedly an easy jaunt, Bob had unfortunately forgotten to take his well-worn army issue canvas, high ankle, rigid, rubber-soled jungle boots up to Vanimo. He was issued a new pair from the QM store the day before the patrol set off. This was a bad mistake as it usually took a few weeks to wear in a new pair of jungle boots. After six hours of walking along the beach, Bob had a serious case of blisters. On the second day these were raw and bleeding and on the third day he had to continue along the beach in socks. At the Mission he was able to bathe his feet in salt water and the blisters started to heal. The Lieutenant leading the patrol wisely appointed Bob as signals officer, and he was able to stay at the Mission while patrols went out each day to visit inland villages. The other memory Bob has of this patrol was the horrible smell of flying foxes being cooked by soldiers for their supper. Bob declined the offer of flying fox stew. Then in a moment of pure luck, a large double-hulled lakatoi with a seriously big outboard motor arrived at the Mission. It had been sent down the coast to bring the patrol back to Vanimo. Bob was saved from the ordeal of walking home. The patrol finally arrived back at 11pm at night after surviving a broken-down motor and nearly being swamped by huge waves as the powerless lakatoi drifted towards the beach. In the Army, getting blisters was a chargeable offence so Bob had to face the indignity of being treated at the medical centre and then facing a barrage of insults from the most senior NCO at Vanimo for being a weak Nasho, not looking after himself and not getting an issue of boots well before the patrol.

The Mission and a small landing strip are still located at Leitre, about halfway along the straight black sand beach between Vanimo and Sissano Lagoon. In 1998, this area was devastated by a tragic tsunami that hit the low-lying Aitape coast villages and caused more than 3000 deaths and thousands of casualties.

A close encounter of the dangerous kind happened while John was attached to a platoon on a "show the flag" patrol to remote villages along the coast between Vanimo and Aitape. The patrol had stopped for the night on a sand dune forming a strip of level land between the ocean and a lagoon. While camp was being set up, John wandered off to wash his sweaty body in the peaceful lagoon. As soon as John immersed himself and started to splash around, a soldier raced up and urged him to get out of the water. John obeyed and when asked what the problem was the soldier pointed to drag marks in the sand between the ocean and the lagoon where John had been splashing about and said "puk puk I stap". John had been about to share the lagoon with one or more notoriously dangerous and huge saltwater crocodiles. Much chastened, John found the soldiers stringing up hammocks quite high between the palm trees and realised why they would not be sleeping on the ground that night.

Rick enjoyed patrols because the soldiers insisted that he speak *tok pisin*, a break from the requirement to use English in the classroom. Rick's most memorable patrol was with an Infantry platoon to the villages of Pagei, Amoi, Nambis and Ossima near the Indonesian border. This seemed a hard slog at the time, even for a fit twenty-year-old. The Pagei patrol post had been opened in secret in 1963 to observe the border and monitor potential tensions between TPNG and Indonesia. The jungle had been cleared and the timber used to build the patrol post and a government school. There was little else there in 1967 apart from the landing strip, although there was a Christian influence. Missionaries had sub-divided the territory and in Pagei's case, one side of the airstrip was Catholic territory and the other Seventh Day Adventist. Being close to the border a lookout was kept for infiltrators from Irian Jaya as there were supplies of value at Pagei such as food and water and an airstrip and accommodation, all likely to be commandeered if Indonesian military patrols crossed the border. The patrol did have some down-time and Rick took an opportunity, with a guide, to divert to other villages along the way. One was Issi village which, as Rick recollects, was on two sites and hence there was an Issi 1 and an Issi 2. Villagers would occasionally be passed along a track, usually in a family group, with the man in front with a machete and a woman behind carrying everything else. Her *bilum*, or bag woven from local material, usually contained yams, kau-kau and sweet potatoes and often a child. The *bilum* strap was across the forehead and hung down over her back, freeing the hands to carry even more. Generally, the local guides had difficulty in expressing in English, or even *tok pisin*, the distances between places or of the time it would take to reach the next point along the track. No one had a wristwatch and so it was complicated if asking, for example, "What time will we reach Issi?" You could ask, but the response would generally come in two forms. One was by a villager pointing to the sun and then lowering his hand to indicate where it would be positioned on arrival: "wanem san i long hap" (meaning, "when the sun is here".) The other was an description of distance as in "lik-lik tasol" (not far) or "long way lik-lik" (far but not a long way) meaning a hundred metres, or possibly up to five kilometres!

Access to Pagei in 1966 was by a fifteen-minute flight from Vanimo. The difficulty of travelling overland was demonstrated when an Australian teacher at Pagei, Trevor Freestone, traversed the jungles and ranges and walked a group of his older Primary School children, with guides, on a two day trek to Vanimo to participate in a sports carnival. They won the Marching Competition. The Pagei children did not enjoy the same protein diet as their coastal schoolmates as their staple food was sago and they were less well-nourished and therefore less competitive in sports, but they did get their first opportunity to see the ocean, cars and ships and they got to eat fresh fish before returning home. Remarkably Rick, who visited Trevor's classroom in Pagei during a patrol in 1966, came in contact with Trevor once again in April 2018, with Trevor then 76 and Rick heading towards 73 years. Trevor gave permission for the following description of Pagei to be included:

"The Australian government sent in patrols and convinced the villagers on the border to move close to Pagei patrol post where they could be closely watched and not influenced by Indonesia. They established five villages, Nambis being one. This made it possible to establish Pagei Primary School with enough children to make it viable. It was also easier to provide medical aid. It also provided a work force capable of clearing a large enough area in the rain forest to establish Pagei base and airstrip. Bob O'Connell was the patrol officer who achieved this amazing task. They disassembled a sawmill and had carriers carry this in, piece by piece from the coast, then reassemble it to enable them to cut the logs created by the clearing process. This timber was then

used to build the patrol officers' house, my house, and the aid post. They also cut the timber to build the school class rooms. The same thing with the tractor, each part carried in piece by piece then reassembled. The tractor then helped construct the airfield. No helicopters were anywhere to be seen. When one walked through the thick rain forest you could appreciate the enormity of this task.

In 1966, there were only two Australians based there, the patrol officer and myself. I had two New Guinean teachers to assist me. In 1967, they brought in an Australian Federal Police officer whose task was to interview the ever-increasing number of refugees coming across the border trying to escape the Indonesian Army. Their tales were horrific. They were not allowed to stay and were sent back. However, as they knew they would be killed if they returned, they secretly set up their own village hidden in the jungle. They had no services and life was difficult to say the least. My students knew about the camp and secretly took me to visit. Luckily, the children could communicate with the group. We took a quantity of food to give away. The refugees were very suspicious of our reason for being there and were happy to see us leave. I never told anyone of this visit. Even today the Indonesians are treating the West Papuans horribly, and the Australian Government who are aware of this choose to do nothing. I wrote to the Foreign Affairs Minister who admitted she knew about the way the Indonesians were treating the West Papuans and said she would raise the matter with them when she visited Indonesia. A short time later she did visit and from the news reports I saw she congratulated the Indonesians on the way they were handling the West Papuan problem. I am still disgusted and hope the West Papuan movement is finally able to convince the United Nations to give them Independence. Pagei, along with Green River, was the most isolated place in TPNG. Pagei was considered isolated due to the fact that its only access was by air, and the short strip was often closed due to the weather."

Laurie's first patrol was for two-weeks with 1 Platoon, B Coy, while he was posted at Vanimo. It was led by Lt Radcliffe, Sergeant Kripakia and Laurie, and consisted of a platoon of twenty-five soldiers. The task was to patrol from Amanab to Imonda along the Indonesian border surveying the terrain and visiting villages and reporting on the inhabitants. The patrol began with a flight to Amanab in two Caribou aircraft on a day like most in New Guinea, with heavy cloud cover. Laurie loved the Caribou. The flight as usual involved dodging in and out of clouds trying to follow a route across the rugged mountainous terrain below. All flying was visual only. After a descent through a gap in the clouds into the wrong location, the Caribou were trapped in a deep valley and the only way out was on full throttle spiralling back up through the same hole in the cloud they had just come through. Most of the troops were sick and the atmosphere was unpleasant. The eventual arrival was no less spectacular as a tiny runway appeared and it seemed to begin at the edge of a cliff. Safely landed, the patrol set out immediately. Each day they had set destinations, visiting the small village populations along the route.

The NCO's and platoon commander always carried a loaded firearm, and the soldiers had a loaded magazine in their kit. Rations were "PI packs" (known as 'Native pack') and consisted of a tin of bully beef, packets of dried cabbage or carrot which was VERY salty, a packet of brown rice, dried biscuits with a container of jam, some tea or coffee and a tube of condensed milk.

Each soldier had two packs per day and although they were a bit meagre, Laurie initially thought they were not too bad, but by day two he was hungry and by day three he was starving. Only another 11 days to go! When the patrol started Laurie was 80kg and on return he was 70kg. Along the way the patrol was expected to supplement their diet with whatever could be paid for or bartered with villagers, such as fruit, eggs, sago, sweet potato, pineapples, and coconuts. Trading this fresh food for items from ration packs was allowed. Clean water was always a problem, and the chlorine tablets left a distinctive taste in food. The walking part of the patrol was no picnic either. The jungle was thick, very thick in places. When the track was not going straight up, they were invariably going straight down and generally there was a raging stream to be traversed at the bottom of each slope, often involving a balancing act on wet and unstable log bridges. The tracks were reasonably well defined, but Laurie was glad he was not doing the navigating. A couple of the large villages had some sort of administration presence, but most were small hamlets.

Then there were the little critters. Everywhere clouds of mosquitoes seemed oblivious to repellent, which was liberally applied, but soon sweated off. With the water also came leeches which generally stayed around the tops of boots and socks but the more adventurous migrated further up the leg to the nether regions. Getting rid of leeches was the first task each time a patrol stopped for a ten-minute break and usually the hot tip of a cigarette or match would do the trick. Added to that discomfort was the chafing from the pack and rifle and the unsettling effect of ration packs mixed with local food on a sensitive "European" stomach. At the end of each day Laurie was exhausted. His bed was a simple affair constructed with a machete wielded by

Private Willy, one of Laurie's favourite soldiers, who simply volunteered himself as Laurie's guardian. Two sharpened crossed poles in the ground supported the stick bed frame with a "Cape, Half Man, Shelter" draped above for weather protection. A mosquito net provided a challenge to the mozzie swarms, but a surprising number had no problem getting through.

Patrols were resupplied by an air drop from a Pilatus Porter light plane, usually aimed at an open square in a small village. If the drop was in a jungle clearing this usually required clearing some trees with axes and machetes but even so it was still a rather dicey sort of a drop zone. The Porter had good low speed capability, but the approaches had to be at high level and each drop ended spectacularly with everything scattered far and wide. Most of the ration packs survived along with the special canisters containing mail and things secreted before the patrol such as special treats and cigarettes. Unfortunately, the hexamine cube, a condensed fuel substitute, used for fire lighting and cooking, did not fare well and usually shattered on impact so they had to be rationed.

When the patrol arrived at Imonda village, Lt Radcliffe came down with a severe stomach and bowel condition which left him immobilised. He had intended to lead half of the platoon the next morning to a village just on the TPNG side of the border, so instead Laurie was deputised with Sgt Kripakia to lead a section (of five soldiers) on a trek of about 8km through rugged country. Without packs they made good time. The track wound up and down over creek crossings until they could see a village through the trees on the other side of a valley. To their surprise there was an Indonesian flag flying from a flagpole. This set a few alarm bells going and Sgt Kripakia ordered the men to change magazines to live rounds before they proceeded cautiously for the next kilometre. By the time the patrol crested the rise into the village the flag was gone – the villagers had worked out the strangers were a TPNG Army patrol. The arrival of fully armed 2PIR soldiers was persuasive and after some heated *tok pisin* the flag was produced. It turned out that an Indonesian military patrol had visited the village only a few hours before and ordered the flag be flown. The border was still being reviewed in 1966 by Australia and Indonesia so it was not clear if this village belonged on the Australian side of the border. To this day Laurie wonders what might have happened if the 2PIR patrol had arrived when the Indonesian patrol was still in the village. Could it have been an incident to spark conflict with Indonesia in the tense international geopolitics of the late 1960s? Laurie's patrol returned to Imonda with the flag as evidence and a formal report was sent in as required, but Laurie never found out what happened to the report, or the flag. International diplomacy and military strategy were not the lot of a lowly Education Sergeant.

The most unusual off-base military experience involved two Army Land Rovers taking a soldier's corpse for burial in his home village inland along the Wewak-Maprik road. Max had been deputised to take photographs of the ceremony in the village. The Maprik road was half a metre deep in mud most of the way so after eight hours slow progress it was late afternoon when the two vehicles reached the soldier's village. In the coffin, the ice packing around the body had melted and there was strong odour of decay by the time the body was delivered to the large local Catholic Church run by an American Missionary, two Sisters and eight local pastors. The Mission had been there for six years and the two Sisters had not seen Wewak at all, going straight from the USA to the village. There was an hour of crying and singing and then with a 2PIR Piper playing a dirge, an amazingly incongruous ritual in a remote village, the coffin was carried to the soldier's brother's house to be buried the following day. The two vehicles set off back to Wewak at a dangerously fast pace, getting bogged only once and arriving late at night after some hair-raising manoeuvres by the drivers who were not keen to spend a night camped somewhere along the road. As the sun had dried much of the mud, the trip back only took three hours.

Bob also went on bivouac to the PIR base at Mt Hagen in the Highlands. Bob soon realised why Mt Hagen was a popular destination for expatriates. It was high up in the ranges with cool sunny days and cooler misty nights, quite a break from the oppressive heat and humidity of the tropical coast. The Army maintained a small camp at Mt Hagen for Militia (Volunteer) training purposes. Bob's role on the bivouac was to train soldiers in the use of the Browning automatic pistol as well as the FI carbine which was replacing the WWII Owen Machine Gun. The Browning was a fine weapon, but it was virtually impossible to put two rounds into the same spot. Training consisted of Bob repeating what he had read in the manuals, and then a Corporal translating in *tok pisin*. There were three days set aside for instruction. On the allotted day for testing, thousands of rounds of FI and Browning rounds were fired into and around the targets. The training schedule was not too onerous, and Bob had a good look at the prosperous agricultural valleys and the town of Mt Hagen, a small but bustling Highland's centre. The roads were gravel and poorly maintained and getting from the camp into town involved crossing quite a deep ford, also used by expats and locals for washing their vehicles. The poor state of the roads was addressed by groups of local people clearing boulders and filling potholes. This seemed to be a widespread and constant task, which Bob reasoned was set by the Australian colonial administration as a useful task for local people. Their equipment was basic with hoes, picks, and shovels and not a single piece of road making machinery in sight.

Max went to the Mt Hagen camp for a similar rifle company training exercise but had the misfortune to drive a land rover into a deep ravine while taking a short cut across a field of two-metre high kunai grass. Later, Max, Kerry Dohring (one of the new Nasho Chalkies) and WO2 Paulius (from Buka) took leave and went to Mt Hagen for the 1967 Mt Hagen Show, an annual event shared with Goroka in alternative years. This was quite a spectacle with tens of thousands of highlanders yelling, thumping drums and dressed in amazing costumes and headdresses, dancing for days around the showgrounds. This was the New Guinea version of the popular Agricultural Shows days held in most Australian country towns and capital cities. The Show included a 'Ball' and the usual array of agricultural produce and equipment. In 1967, thirty-eight DC-3 charters landed at the airstrip plus a hundred arrivals by smaller planes. Max was impressed with the huge crowds of Highlanders, women wearing only a leaf tucked into a belt, and fierce looking men mostly with beards. He wrote to his parents that the Highlands were the "richest area in the Territory ... this is a paradox of the Territory and is something that will cause trouble when independence comes. All the wealth of the country is in the Highlands, but the coastal people have all the brains and know how". (Luckily, this naïve prediction did not prove to be entirely correct.) The Mt Hagen and Goroka shows continue today as an international tourism event.Later in life the

Nasho Six often reflected on how being in the jungle in New Guinea had affected Australian soldiers who fought during WWII, but this had not been a topic of conversation in 1966-1967, despite only being two decades after the war and the Nasho Six occupying what was a former Japanese base. All six Nashos agree that patrolling added an incredibly special experience in the formative stages of their lives.

30. Army survey map of 1966 showing route of Max's four week patrol, 19.11.1966 – 16.12.1967. The heavy black line was the route taken. The Indonesian border is along the left margin of the map.

CHAPTER NINE

ORDERLY SERGEANT DUTY

Sometimes the Nasho Chalkie Sergeants had to live up to the masquerade that they were real soldiers. This mostly became apparent when rostered for a 24-hour stint as Duty Sergeant, also known as Orderly Sergeant. Sergeants punished for misdemeanours were rostered on as Duty Sergeant. There was also a duty Platoon on standby in case of emergency (or attack) as well as for patrolling the Barrack's perimeter and grounds. The main role of the Duty Sergeant was to inspect the preparedness of the Duty Platoon and supervise their patrolling, and to punish those soldiers on CB – confined to barracks for minor demeanours - with an hour of marching and rifle drill on the Parade Ground each morning and evening, with commands barked out by the Orderly Sergeant.

Soldiers on CB had usually committed a minor offence such as being drunk in the OR's canteen, dropping their rifle or not being quick enough to respond to a command by an Officer or Sergeant. They had to wear full uniform, with full pack and rifle and report five times a day to the Orderly or Duty Sergeant to show they were on the base and following orders. CB also meant soldiers could not visit the OR's bar or leave the camp. Those on CB had to report with full pack, rifle and immaculate uniform and shiny boots and form ranks on the parade ground for their 60 minutes of drill at dawn and dusk. Orderly Sergeants also were tasked with the standard Army routine of taking down the flag each evening and raising it again the next morning. Max recalls only doing a few Duty Sergeants, while Laurie claims he copped it sweet just about every weekend. One of these surely was the result of a phone call direct from the Lt Colonel to Laurie while he was having breakfast.

The Lt Colonel demanded to know why the regimental flag was flying upside down, in Army protocol, a distress call! Laurie had not noticed this when raising the flag earlier that morning. Max copped two Duty Sergeants for sitting in the *haus win* with his foot resting 50cm up on a roof support pole. This was deemed inappropriate behaviour. Another Max misdemeanour was riding his Moped home in the rain from training a girls' basketball team in town, wearing only a raincoat and shorts. This was after 6.30pm, when regulations to prevent Malaria deemed you had to be wearing long sleeves and long pants. Max flew through the Main gate, bare legs and coat flapping in the rain and copped an extra duty.

There was a Duty Officer and a Duty Sergeant rostered on every day and they had to complete all their normal tasks. A day started at 5.30am, woken by the preceding days Duty Sergeant, quickly don full parade uniform and scoot down to the parade ground to raise the Regimental Flag, followed by an hour's drill for any soldiers on CB. The Education Nashos, who barely considered themselves to be real soldiers, therefore had somewhat of an aversion to anything involving discipline, strict routine, or anything vaguely regimental. However, at 6am they would be at the Regimental flagpole checking the list of soldiers on CB to make sure all had reported in for their punishment and then barking commands to "about turn, present rifle, down rifle, strip rifle, reassemble, attention, right dress, about turn, march," repeated possibly thirty or forty times, but done according to the book in case an Officer or the dreaded RSM happened to pass by. Any incidents reported by the Duty Platoon from the night before had to be investigated and a report passed on further up the line to the Military Police if it was serious.

The early morning duty having been accomplished it was time for breakfast at the Sergeants' Mess. After a quick inspection of the Platoon to take up the next Duty Platoon role, it was time to head along to the Education Centre for a day's classes. At 1.00pm the CB roll was checked again along with another gear inspection. After lunch at the Sergeants Mess it was back to classes. The roll-taking and inspection of those on CB was repeated at 4pm, 6pm and 9pm. Before 6pm the Duty Sergeant had to rig up their donga with mosquito net, in the Guard House before changing to night uniform.

The 9pm roll call was the end of day for those on CB but not for the Duty Sergeant, as it was the start of an uncomfortable night bunked in the guardhouse. Sleep was limited as either the Duty Officer, or Duty Sergeant had to be on call, which usually involved a gentleman's agreement about who would take first sleep (of 3 hours) and who would take first watch. The first watch also involved a routine wander through the OR's mess and kitchens and a chance to grab a quick coffee. The morning brought the suffering Duty Sergeant full circle, and the role was passed over to the next in line.

Rick recalls that being in the second *sak-sak* row of sleeping quarters was one reason for his doing fewer orderly sergeant duties than Laurie. Rick's room was not on the RSM's walking route along the front row to the Mess which meant he could spot gear that had not been properly stowed, or a Sergeant who was a little tardy at getting out of bed or tidying their donga.

Fortunately for Duty Sergeants, Moem was rather quiet and there were only a few incidents that required more than a cursory glance or a "Front and centre soldier" to find out what was going on. Max recalls a soldier who failed to turn up for his "CB" drill. Inquiries revealed he had a "leg problem" and wanted to go home. Further failures to turn up for drill, meant he was then charged and put in the camp lock-up for the night. Max complained to everyone in the Mess because it meant attending a formal hearing before the soldier's Company CO the next morning.

Bob recalls one night when a group of drunk soldiers went on a rampage at the OR's canteen (or bar) at Moem and were smashing bottles and threatening the bar staff. Two military Police, the Duty Sergeant and a full platoon descended on the OR's canteen and arrested the drunken soldiers and closed the bar. These soldiers were later court-martialled and cashiered out of the Army and a quiet peace returned to the Barracks. In two years, there were few incidents of this nature. Usually, the Military Police handled domestic disputes and personal matters leaving the perimeter patrolling and check on buildings to the Duty Platoon.

Because of its twenty-four-hour, mundane, rigorous attention to protocol, in full dress uniform, the Nasho Six quickly realised that Duty Sergeant was a task to be avoided. Clearly this was a role that was never volunteered for and especially avoided at weekends. As readers might imagine all this military behaviour was regarded as well beyond the call of duty and loyalty to nation required of Education Nashos, who after all were only schoolteachers in fancy dress pretending to be Sergeants.

31. Laurie and Lt Peter Radcliffe with a fish bought from a passing lakatoi at Vanimo.

32. The beach front and Mess at Vanimo, taken from a visiting LSM, run up on the beach.

CHAPTER TEN

VANIMO

Vanimo base camp, near the Indonesian border, was Shangri-La. For the Chalkie sergeants, apart from a few education classes, an occasional duty as Orderly Sergeant and doing the daily weather reports, there was not much else to do except for golf, water skiing and a fair bit of reading, with a lakatoi trip across the bay to the Catholic Mission the major highlight. Vanimo Barracks was a dream posting. The infantry Company stationed there for a three-month posting required only a minimum education presence and because the soldiers were often off-base patrolling or on exercises the teaching load was light. Laurie had been sent to Vanimo immediately on arriving at 2PIR and was then followed by Peter who unfortunately contacted hepatitis at Vanimo and was airlifted back to Wewak. Bob and John were sent up as temporary replacements. At various stages most of the Education Sergeants visited Vanimo for short courses or if they could arrange it, a "swan" on the Caribou supply run. Vanimo was essentially a training camp and doubled as a strategic outpost close to the Irian Jaya border. The support staff at Vanimo was limited to a few caterers, mechanics, signalmen and clerks. It was also a point from which patrols could be made deeper into the West Sepik interior.

The Mess at Vanimo was shared by Officers and Sergeants and overlooked a curving bay with two small volcanic outcrops about a kilometre offshore. On the northern seaward perimeter (no fences) a wide flat spit joined to a tombola or raised rock outcrop which formed a peninsula around which the few public buildings of Vanimo clustered. Between the camp and the town was an unused grass landing strip which ran from the sea on one side of the peninsula to the other. On the landward side of the camp was a new gravel landing strip that was longer and ran along the extent of the camp. The camp nestled under coconut palms and being nearly surrounded by the sea was a cool and breezy environment.

Laurie as the first posted to Vanimo hardly had time to pack, find out what he was to do and prepare for courses. He really was on his own. The flight to Vanimo was Laurie's initiation into the workhorse of the Army, the De Havilland DCH-4 Caribou. They could carry a fully equipped platoon, were very noisy to fly in but superbly suited to the short airstrips and rugged, mountainous countryside of New Guinea. Their Pratt and Whitney radial engines were extremely powerful, and they had fantastic take-off and landing capabilities. As twenty-year old Aussies this was exciting, and everyone loved flying in them and whenever possible took a "swan".

In 1966, it was only twenty years since the Second World War had finished. On Laurie's first low level flight from Wewak to Vanimo he noticed visible signs of the war everywhere. Wrecked vessels were in the water, bits and pieces of wrecked machinery were overgrown with vegetation and bomb craters pockmarked wartime airstrips along the Aitape coast. This was a reminder to everyone just how close the war had been to Australia.

Laurie thought Vanimo was like a picture postcard. The allocated Education Sergeant's bedroom looked out on to the disused grass runway. The view eastward was to a beautiful, curving, tropical palm-lined beach with turquoise blue water.

The disused grass airstrip separated the barracks from the few stores, government offices, primary school, a tavern with limited accommodation, jetties with outhouses perched at the end that served as toilets, a market area open on weekends and a small prison enclosure made of loose wire and bamboo – hardly maximum security. This collection of buildings was the grandiosely named town of Vanimo. The Army and the town lived side by side, usually in a harmonious relationship. There was a very friendly relationship with the locals and some lively sessions at the local tavern, known as "The Club", which was a great place to make contacts. There were bush pilots like the mad Scotsman "Scottie", the local doctor, George Melafont, who invited Laurie to Christmas lunch, the guest house owner, Gordon Campbell, and the club was the stopping point for the Kiaps (Administration Patrol Officers) when they came into Vanimo. Unfortunately, for later rotations of Chalkies, the tavern was declared out-of-bounds after a couple of incidents.

Setting up an education course at Vanimo was a challenge as there was little in the way of resources and soldiers were constantly coming and going. Communication with home base at Moem barracks was mostly by snail mail. The only available teaching space was the OR's mess or dining room but often classes were taken outside under the palm trees.

Apart from education, organising sport and running the Sergeants Mess bar, the Education Sergeant also had other duties such as recording the weather twice a day and reporting in using the short-wave radio. This involved taking the daily meteorological readings for temperature, wind direction, humidity, cloud cover and rainfall and then making a radio call to Wewak to report the day's figures. The weather report also included commentary on the status of the surface of the gravel landing strip in case it was unusable due to heavy rains, especially important for heavy Hercules transport landings.

Down behind the radio shack was a shed which had various pieces of equipment including a Land Rover with something that looked like a canon mounted on top. Laurie liked mucking around with mechanical things and found it a bit intriguing. The company quartermaster explained that this vehicle had been there quite a while and nobody really knew how it worked, but it needed cleaning and asked Laurie to have a go. The mounted cannon turned out to be a 105mm recoilless rifle designed to fire an anti-tank projectile. By trial and error, it was not too difficult to work out how to strip it down, clean and assemble it, which Laurie was asked to do several times. After his return to Moem Barracks, Laurie was summoned by WO2 Keith Payne to Admin HQ. Keith Payne (later a VC winner in Vietnam) was renowned as a curt character and not overly friendly towards Nasho Sergeants. Laurie thought he was in trouble. WO2 Payne asked, "What's this I hear about you playing around with the 105 in Vanimo?" When Laurie explained his tinkering at Vanimo, he was told there were several 105mm at Moem at the transport depot and they were just sitting there because no-one knew much about them. Thus, a teacher-trained, half-trained artilleryman and wanna-be backyard mechanic and Nasho Sergeant was ordered to prepare an instruction course and teach a squad to dismantle and assemble the 105mms, which he did. There were no written instructions that he could find anywhere so Laurie made up his own. That put paid to Laurie's assumption that the Army had written procedures and instructions for everything. The 105mms were never fired at Moem during the Nasho's time.

When Laurie was not teaching at Vanimo he had all sorts of other odd duties. One day he was called to help supervise live firing practice at the range on the north side of Vanimo Point with platoon commander Lt Peter Radcliffe. After the exercise they were left with a couple of hundred rounds of ammunition and the Lieutenant said, "We are not taking this back." So, they loaded a few magazines each, set up some targets and borrowed 7.62mm SLR's from some very reluctant diggers. They proceeded to blast off the magazines, from the hip, until the weapons were smoking hot before handing them back to the amused soldiers.

Rick made several trips to Vanimo. He was very prone to sea-sickness and has a memory of an uncomfortable fishing journey with Laurie and others in a large lakatoi. Rick also made frequent trips to and from the Catholic Mission across the bay, where there were several lay people including pilots and nurses. The Mission was reasonably self-sufficient, and there was surf off the point in the Monsoon season. At that time Rick was a churchgoer and was at a midnight mass on Christmas Eve in 1966 at the Vanimo Church, a *haus win* style hut with sand floor, when someone yelled out "snakis" (snake). Never has a church been cleared so quickly. The walk or jog along the beach from the camp to the Mission was beautiful and took 45 minutes. The beach was not wide but fringed with coconut trees. Half-way around the route was interrupted by a picturesque stream under the shade of overhanging branches with water as fresh as could possibly be. No better half-way resting place could be imagined.

On his return to TPNG to work as a civilian, Rick recollects an Ansett-MAL DC-3 flight to Vanimo where he was to assist with a Police training course. Rick was the sole passenger. The plane flew at an altitude of 200 metres along the coast. When the diligent co-pilot came back to offer a "minty", Rick had just noticed sunlight reflections from glistening water some distance inland and asked what it was. "I don't know so let's go look" was the response. The DC-3 did a loop and circuited what was found to be …. a large, flooded sago field; personalised tourism at its best.

Peter headed to Vanimo in March 1967 with A Coy to replace Laurie's B Coy on the next rotation. His duties included the same basic classroom delivery, duty officer, weather reporting and supervising the bar in the combined Officers and Sergeants Mess. In May, Peter took off with a platoon to fly to Telefomin on a remote area exercise which included patrols into the Star Mountains, a part of the massive central cordillera of New Guinea island. Peter acted as load master for the two Caribou and noted a Land Rover formed the load for one of the Caribou. Judiciously, Pete allocated himself to the other Caribou! Telefomin was a real eye-opener. The outlying villages, the indigenous tribal groups, and their isolated way of life, seemed to a young twenty-year-old Australian to confirm the so-called primitive nature of the people, meaning they were allegedly mostly untouched by western influences and only partially in contact with the administration or government. The patrolling and training took place against the background of the majestic Star Mountains. Two days before the patrol ended, Peter became ill and on returning to Vanimo, the doctor at the town medical post diagnosed hepatitis. Peter was then flown to Wewak for a two-week hospital stint after which he was placed on no duties, and then light duties, until he left for Australia in late October 1967.

Bob arrived at Vanimo for his posting with a new LP record player and a stack of classic and pop LPs including Simon and Garfunkel, The Beatles, My Fair Lady soundtrack, and Hell Bent for Leather, among others. In a very welcome change from the *sak-sak* ablutions block at Moem, the showers were fresh water! Another respite for Bob was to arrange a double-hulled lakatoi to sail across the bay to the west of the camp to the Catholic Wirowi Mission. Another diversion was water skiing. During Bob's visit the Company CO (a Major) had become an avid skier but needed a boat driver. It was not unusual towards the end of a lesson for the CO to wander in and point out to Bob that the bay was particularly glassy that afternoon. This was a sign for Bob to end the class promptly, set up the runabout and outboard and have a set of skis waiting. There was always a back-up supply of AV-gas at Vanimo for the use of light planes used for aerial surveying and supply drops. The amount of AV-gas used at Vanimo bore no relation to the frequency of planes landing and taking off and some creative accounting probably disguised the fact that the AV-gas was being used for water sports.

During Bob and John's posting replacing Peter at Vanimo, John as secondary trained, took the advanced courses while Bob who was primary trained, took the basic IOE and PCOE. They claimed that during their posting, Vanimo received its best period of concentrated teaching. Every few weeks one of the Education Corps officers from Moem would arrive on a commercial flight to run the necessary testing. Other Sergeant's duties at Vanimo involved the nightly attendance at a desk in the ORs dining area so that privates and corporals could return books and borrow more from the quite reasonably stocked library. There was a good range of reading levels and borrowing was popular. Bob claimed he read the whole library during his stint at Vanimo. Another duty was to train one of the Lance-Corporals in the operation of a Bell and Howell 16mm film projector. Each Saturday night was movie night and Vanimo, like Moem, relied on 16mm films sent up from Port Moresby. The movie set up at Vanimo was idyllic with an outdoor screen on the edge of the grass landing strip and all ranks brought their own chairs to sit in the open. The movies were usually popular box-office hits from Australia but often ten or more years old. Westerns were clearly the soldiers' favourite and they cheered more for the Indians than the cowboys or cavalry. The musical South Pacific was another favourite.

Unlike Moem, where strict Army protocols prevailed there was a much more relaxed atmosphere at Vanimo. This was engendered mostly by shared morning teas in the combined Officers and Sergeants Mess. The Mess at Vanimo had open sides, with mosquito wire screening and was a pleasant breezy room to share stories over the standard issue scones, cake, and sandwiches. The Company Commander often took the privilege of relating a story from his days in Vietnam and this was always welcomed as it usually forced tea break to run over for an extra fifteen minutes.

Bob relates an incident at Vanimo that ended up with him giving evidence at a Discipline hearing. Bob had been Duty Sergeant with the Duty Platoon on an otherwise quiet night. At Vanimo this was reduced to a section, roughly twelve soldiers under a

Corporal, with either an Officer or Sergeant in the Duty or Orderly role. The routine was much the same as at Moem Barracks with the main difference being that those on CB were excused from marching drills and were sent to help in the kitchen as part of their punishment. One night around 10.30pm after a night drinking spirits with some civilian mates, a drunken Corporal decided to sit out on the grass airstrip mumbling and refusing to go into his barracks. It was already after lights-out. When confronted by Bob and the Duty Platoon. Corporal, he refused to get up. When the two tried to lift him up and direct him back into camp he cursed and lashed out with his fists striking Bob in the chest. Bob wisely withdrew and sought the help of Staff Sergeant Bob Wriggley who turned up with a squad of men and a jeep, into which the drunk was roughly bundled and then driven to the local police lock-up. (Vanimo army base did not have a lock-up.) This particular Corporal had played Aussie Rules with Bob back at Moem and was also in Bob's PCOE class at Vanimo, so when the CO convened a hearing the next day, Bob was feeling unsettled and nervous when called upon to make a report. The charges were read, and the soldier was asked if he understood the three charges – drunk and disorderly, striking a non-commissioned officer and disobeying lawful commands. He apologised and said he was sorry. Bob then gave his evidence, detailed the course of events, noting the strike was not deliberate, and more a reflex action. The CO then dismissed everyone except the accused and proceeded to give the offender a stern lecture on what was expected from Corporals.

The next week, the Corporal returned to his PCOE class as though nothing had ever happened. He was otherwise a fine soldier with an unblemished record and had retained his Corporal stripes, and in a strange turn of events, a month later was remarkably promoted to Sergeant. Back at Moem he strode into the Sergeants' Mess one day showing of his new stripes and introduced himself to Bob, Sergeant to Sergeant. They shared a beer and laughed about that night in Vanimo.

Another memorable occasion at Vanimo involved both John and Bob having to bare their buttocks. This happened in the wake of Peter Suna being airlifted back to Wewak for hospitalization.

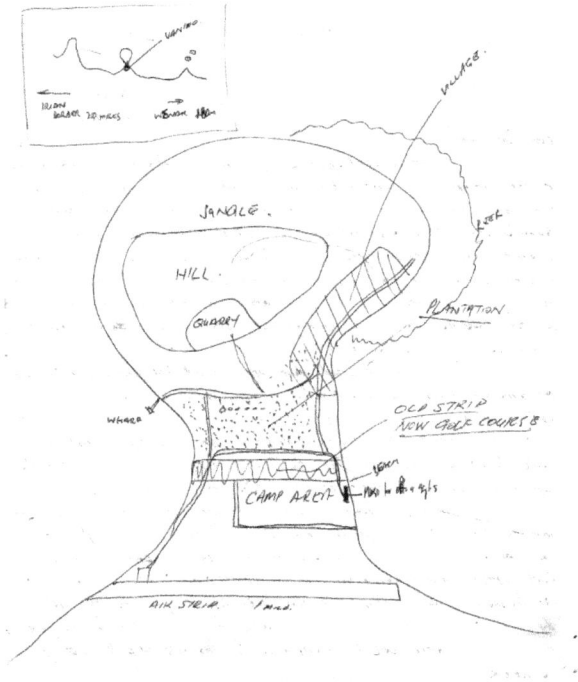

33. Map of Vanimo (Source: map sent home by Max to his parents, August 1966).

One afternoon, unannounced and unexpected, two giant Hercules transport planes buzzed the camp and then landed in perfect formation on the gravel landing strip. The noise was horrendous and the *sak-sak* huts shook. The Hercules was the Army's work horse and with four turbo-prop engines and huge back door and cargo space it could take on an impressive payload. As soon as the massive rear doors were lowered, Land Rovers began towing trailers of gear on to the landing strip followed by two platoons from the Army Medical Corps. Their camp kitchens, marquees, four-man sleeping tents, beds and boxes of mysterious equipment were soon on the ground. The Medicos had landed.

The cause of this dramatic arrival was that back in Australia, in Adelaide, in the wake of Peter's diagnosis, a decision had been made to eliminate hepatitis, and a team was therefore dispatched by air straight to TPNG to analyse, screen and treat the whole Vanimo camp. The Medicos were self-sufficient in a fly-in and fly-out manner and set about their tasks without much interaction with the PIR. Casual conversations revealed their task was to identify the source of any hepatitis infection, and they began poking around in the sewerage, rubbish, water supply, waste disposal, kitchens, showers, toilets, food stores, refrigerators, and all living quarters.

Bob met up with the medical team twice during their visit. The first was after the camp CO ordered him to set up the water-skiing gear and offer some basic instruction so the medical team could enjoy a break at the weekend. This was a great success with both hopeless beginners and the more experienced laughing and enjoying their way through a weekend's skiing. The second occasion was less pleasant when everyone had to line up and drop their pants and receive a monster needle of gamagobulin, one in

34. Vanimo Parade ground on the disused grass airstrip (set up for movie nights).

35. Peter (left) and John (middle) taking a lakatoi across the bay to Wirowi Mission. Most lakatoi in TPNG by this time were driven by outboard motors.

each buttock as part of the hepatitis investigation. It hurt and certainly was not hilarious. The breakthrough came when the rotting seaweed that littered the beach outside the camp was noticed and it was found to be a breeding place for flies. A clean up removed the rotting seaweed and flies and it was agreed in the Mess that the problem had been solved. However, the report of the medical mission was never seen by anyone at Vanimo so perhaps the flies may not have been the culprit. In two weeks, the investigation was judged to be complete, and the Medicos roared off into the skies.

A sojourn at Vanimo always involved an outboard-powered canoe trip across the bay to the Catholic Mission to visit John's Uncle, Bishop Pascal Sweeney. Max wrote home that Bishop Pascal was, "a very jolly fellow and a down to heart, real Missionary. The Catholic Mission teaches 600 children from around Vanimo and as far south as Telefomin in the central ranges. The Missions are doing a fantastic job in this country and the change from head-hunter to semi-civilised is largely their doing" (with apologies for the 1960s terminology).

One day when off duty from his teaching, John decided to visit his uncle. As no boats were available to hire, and it was a lovely day, John decided to walk the five km around the shoreline. About halfway around there was a watercourse flowing into the bay. This was usually shallow and about ten metres wide but due to heavy rain in previous days, it had doubled in width with dirty moving water coming down the creek and was reasonably deep in the middle, about a metre. Stripping down to his undies, John started across. Halfway, out of the corner of his eye and about ten metres away, a dark, glistening fin broke the surface of the water. With heart in mouth, John froze and for a few seconds fateful thoughts flashed across his mind. And then the curved back and dorsal fin of a dolphin broke the surface and John gasped and remembered to breathe again. John continued, rather hastily, to the far side and after visiting the Mission caught a boat back to Camp.

Vanimo remains a fond memory for all who served there in those happy days broken only by visits by the Navy's LSM landing craft Arundel White and training ship HMAS Anzac, by the noisy landing of Caribou and Hercules on the adjacent gravel strip, and by the regular coming and going of commercial flights and light aircraft from Missionary Aviation. Vanimo was also the take-off point for infantry platoons heading out to patrol along the border, but that is another story.

An infantry Company is still posted on a three-month rotation at Vanimo.

36. Peter, Bishop Pascal Sweeney (John's uncle), John and Bob posing outside the new church at Wirowi Catholic Mission, Vanimo, 1967.

CHAPTER ELEVEN

DINING-IN NIGHTS, SMORGASBORD and AMAZING FISH STEAKS

Sergeants who lived in the *sak-sak* quarters ate in the Dining Room of the *sak-sak* Sergeants Mess. On the western side of camp, the Locally Enlisted Personnel and Australian NCOs lived in their Married Quarters and ate in their homes with their families. Or at least they did until the arrival of "DH", or Regimental Sergeant Major Darryl Howells. In a moment of epiphany, the new RSM insisted that every Non-Commissioned Officer (NCOs) must attend a monthly Dining-In Night. This involved about fifty men in formal Dress Uniform, with tables set with the Regimental cutlery, crystal, silver, and china, much like a very classy wedding back home. Each setting had an array of five wine glasses. The Nasho Six felt they could have been in the swankiest hotel back home. It was a hierarchical thing in the Services to cluster together in an exclusive, ritualistic manner, theoretically to reinforce status, loyalty, and camaraderie. However, dining-in nights were also a fun and military matters took second place when the after-dinner port arrived.

There were rules of engagement, a necessary military procedure. Rule 1: Once seated, no one was permitted to leave the table for any reason. Rule 2: Flagons of port to close the dinner had to be passed from man to man and after pouring your own glass moved on around the table without being set down. Rule 3: Regimental attire of formal evening wear and matching cummerbund, starched white dress shirt and bow tie, or tie was compulsory. Of course, unbelievably shiny black shoes were compulsory. Was this the British Raj in 19th Century India, or TPNG in 1966?

All Sergeants, Warrant Officers and Sergeant-Majors were expected to be in the Mess in formal attire around 6.30pm for nibbles and drinks and half an hour of socialising. Sadly, the intrepid six were not aware of what was to follow and on their first Dining-In night they charged at the bar for free drinks. At 7pm the RSM rang a small bell and declared, "Gentlemen your presence is required. Formal dining has now commenced". Everyone then headed in military fashion to the tables. Stewards crisply hovered around filling wine glasses with excellent Australian wines. Once all were seated and the first round of drinks poured the RSM would clink his glass for silence, deliver a short Regimental pep-talk and say Grace. Entrée followed, often including crayfish or South African cod. This was delicious tucker. Before main course, a senior Warrant Officer would stand and give a short talk, often hilarious and boosting camaraderie. Main course included fish, pork, beef, chicken and often turkey. The waiters (soldiers seconded as stewards) hovered around silently and effectively kept glasses fully primed. These were expensive and trendy reds the quality of which passed un-noticed by the untutored Nasho Six who drank on unaware of the natural bodily consequences to follow. When two hours had passed the popular

NASA launch phrase of the time, "Houston we have a problem," became significant.

Let us remember Rule I: No one stands or leaves the table. But nature calls and full bladders must be emptied. Rumour was that some just sat there too afraid to leave and so pissed their own pants. Others were rumoured to have urinated down the leg of the table. The trick of course, learnt slowly by the Nasho Six, was to tipple less during pre-dinner drinks. So, the RSM just sat there while 50 men started to wriggle and squirm. Sergeant Bowman's plan was to merely slip under the table and then crawl out into the darkness. Sadly, the ever alert RSM spotted said sergeant, and Laurie notched up a few more Duty Sergeant Weekends. As the RSM put it, this was "prejudicial to good order and military discipline!" Good try Laurie!

Finally, relief for all came when the RSM would announce a ten-minute toilet break. The stampede was worth seeing. The last formality was a closing speech by the RSM about military matters accompanied by passing around the carafes of port without touching the table, another quirky regimental custom. Empty carafes were immediately refilled. This was heady stuff for six inexperienced drinkers. At 11pm dinner was declared to be over, and the married sergeants returned to their married quarters, single men walked woozily next door to their donga, and a few hardy souls adjourned to the Mess for a night cap. There were no sickies allowed the next day. Dining-In was lots of fun and the formality was a wonderful experience. The cost of running these nights with imported wines and food must have been considerable, and the bar bill alone would have been impressive. But the Army that eats well fights well, so the Nasho Six took it in their stride. Gradually they learned the smart approach to Dining-In; take one drink only at the pre-dinner soiree, and never empty your wine glass at the table because it would refill before you could turn around.

Eating was always on everyone's mind. Monday to Friday was typically devoted to quick meals between military duties, but on Saturday attention switched to that magical word; "Smorgasbord". Saturdays usually involved a dip in the ocean, ten metres from the bedrooms, and perhaps a road trip into Wewak to post letters and do some shopping in the Chinese trade stores. But everyone was always back by midday for the Sergeants Mess Smorgasbord. This buffet-style concept was rather new in 1966 and of course Army catering did a smorgasbord to its most fulsome extravagance. The quality and quantity were remarkable for a bunch of twenty-year-olds with quiet suburban or rural, outback backgrounds. The grilled mackerel steaks were as big as your hand and 30mm thick; the array of casseroles was amazing and there were mountains of cold meats – beef, lamb, ham, and silverside. There were freshly baked bread rolls on the side and hardly any room on the plate for greens, rice salad, coleslaw, and potato salad. This was seriously like a classy Christmas dinner, and it was presented every Saturday. Piled plates and return trips was standard behaviour, with some disgusting Nasho Sergeants going back for a third helping!!!

Bob had also discovered an ingenious method to score an extra serve at the dining table on normal Mess nights. Ordinary soldiers, with limited English skills, were rostered as waiters and took orders using numbers on a printed menu. A typical call was "Number five, thanks Wamp". (Wamp was a pleasant fellow and one of our students, but a slow waiter who could just handle the menu numbering system.) So, Bob would say he did not want first course, soup, and would be served one of the main course meals. Bob would then enjoy this choice, quickly slip the cutlery to the side, and then when waiters came to collect the other diner's soup plates, he would say that he had changed his mind and would order soup. After soup the waiter, usually a different one, would come back and Bob would then order another main course and follow up with dessert. The WO Caterer never noticed this trick, and the rest of the Mess merely wondered where Bob put all this food. At the farewell party before the six returned to Australia, Bob owned up to this ruse and the WO Caterer admitted he often wondered why there was one extra meal more than the number of Sergeants dining in.

The Education Sergeants typically headed for a Saturday and Sunday afternoon nap around 2pm, followed by another swim and then start again – dinner in the Mess at 6pm and Saturday night movies. Saturdays and Sundays were regarded as the best days of the week.

Sergeants Mess rules were relaxed a little on Sundays allowing for a sleep-in if not rostered as Duty Sergeant. Breakfast on Sundays was at the gentlemanly hour of 8.30am. Any Sunday activity such as making tapes to send home, or surfing at Brandi beach, ended well before midday so that everyone could line up for – Sergeants Mess Sunday BBQ. Another institution!! Meat, meat, meat, and meat, with fish steaks, and salads for the rare Sergeant that dared to declare himself a vegetarian. This was a major meat-eating adventure and had to be taken seriously. Bob discovered that the PNG Sergeants preferred fish steaks, so Bob corralled the sausages, and on one occasion was seen working

37. AFL in Wewak 1967. Sgt Bob Wriggley gaol umpiring, TPNG style!!!

38. Peter Suna on Bob Wriggley's Honda at a Brandi v Army AFL game.

his way through eight barbecued pork chops. Bob declared, and all six Nasho Sergeants agreed, that Sunday BBQ was indeed always an amazing spread. Magic!!!

Movies at the Mess were another social highlight each weekend for the Nasho Six. Max was responsible for choosing and ensuring movies arrived by plane from Port Moresby in time for a Saturday night screening. Typically, there was no suitable hall for screening movies; indeed, there was not even a trained projectionist who knew how to handle the large projector and multiple 16mm reels, usually three to a movie. Luckily, someone had thought of a solution, so a permanent white screen was attached to two large poles separated by a roadway about ten metres from the huas win. The large open-sided *haus win* with a concrete floor and thatched roof was perfect for relaxing in the breeze while peering across the road to the screen. All that was required was an extension cord and a Bell and Howell 16mm projector on a trolley. The secret for the Nasho Sergeants was to nip into the bar early and get a cold beer and then quickly claim a comfy chair up front. Normally NCOs and Officers did not socialise, and each had their own Mess and Bar but on movie nights all joined in, with married staff bringing their wives from the housing area. By 7pm it was pitch black and the assigned Corporal started to make noises that the movie would soon start. Everyone settled in. The six Nasho Sergeants were the back-up projector operators and had to handle any technical problems. Being teachers, they were all were familiar back home in Australia with school projectors.

There were usually two "features" starting with a comedy or musical and ending with a drama, war movie or western. During reel changes there was just time to nick back to the Mess bar and get another beer. It was always hot, and even at night the temperature was around 25 degrees. By 11pm it was all over, and the crowd dispersed, chatting about the movie. Wewak was sent whatever movies were on hand in Port Moresby, and these were mostly the movies the Port Moresby barracks did not want to watch. Bob recollects that South Pacific was at the top of his movie list but Saturday night in the *haus win* had an impressive range of Hollywood epics and big box office grossing movies including *The Graduate, Cool Hand Luke, Lawrence of Arabia, Spartacus, Dirty Dozen, Wait Until Dark, The Great Escape, Bonnie and Clyde, Caine Mutiny, Born Free and The Guns of Navarone*. One favourite in 1966, *Planet of the Apes*, amazingly had a series of sequels and prequels running through to the present. Max reviewed all these movies for his parents in his weekly letter back home to Colac in Victoria.

Movies were also screened for ORs the following Thursday at night in a large outdoor open space which was well attended, raucous and at times hilarious as Papua New Guineans seemed to see humour, tragedy, and horror in unexpected parts of each film. The OR audiences showed their appreciation not at the end but in the middle of scenes by clapping, cheering, and shouting at scenes they saw as funny or tragic. Westerns were favourites at the OR screening. Movie nights were free. It cost the Army a considerable amount to ship bulky 16mm movies up from Queensland, and then domestically to fly them up to Moem barracks in Wewak, and to Vanimo, but it was money well spent and provided a huge relief and leisure time for light-hearted fun in a normally strict and rigorous military schedule.

One special Movie night stood out. In 1966, the Victorian Football League (VFL) decided to do a promotional tour of Papua New Guinea to show off "Aussie Rules". Two ex-players and now popular radio and television commentators, ex-Fitzroy ruck men "Butch" Gale and Jack Edwards arrived in Wewak with a full film of the 1966 Grand Final, won with tremendous excitement by St Kilda for their first ever, and still their only flag. Sergeant Bob Wriggley, an ardent and vocal Saints supporter was in his element and claimed to have been responsible for this magical screening at the *haus win*. This was a few months after the last kick win by St Kilda's Barry Breen and to see the whole game from the MCG on 16mm footage was as exciting as it could get in Moem Barracks. Butch and Jack were 'top blokes', Max reported home to his parents, and the two heroes also volunteered to do a footy clinic for PIR soldiers, and this was a huge success.

Darts were a big feature of life in the Sergeants Mess and the Nashos were often rebuked for being too noisy. Equally noisy were the card games of 500, played exuberantly in the lounge area of the bar. Bingo was the usual Friday night activity and was popular with live-in sergeants and married couples who came from the housing area. Max was judged by the RSM to have a light load around camp so was made Treasurer of the Bar, responsible for totalling up everyone's chits, orders, and bar bill, and keeping a close eye on stocks and daily usage. Max took on this role rather half-heartedly and ignored the obvious fact that the use of spirits was far above that recorded in the Bar takings. Max's haphazard auditing and stocktaking meant that by the time the Nasho Six departed the Bar expenses were seriously over the allocated budget. Max was good at sports but clearly hopeless with numbers and accounting. (These and many other over-budget costs being incurred at 2PIR were of course absorbed by the Australian Army, and taxpayers, as part of Australia's colonial responsibility).

Max also noted a ten-metre flat-bottomed aluminium army runabout with a 40hp outboard motor was often pulled up on the beach near the Sergeants quarters. Max commandeered the boat and with his Chinese mates from town, would scoot across the bay to a beach about ten kilometres away to Ferok at the far end of Brandi beach where a decent wave broke onto sand banks at a river mouth. This was possible because there were about ten surfboards around Wewak at this time, including one owned by surly "Reg" who could not surf and rarely lent his board. Max tried in vain to get his parents to send his ten-foot "Gordon Woods" Malibu up from Victoria. Normally the beach out the front of the Mess was dead calm, but in December to March once the Monsoon season began, waves started to break across the reef. Max, Rick, and Pete were soon out body surfing these waves across the jagged reef. On one infamous night the trio went out naked and body-surfed, skimming just over the jagged reef, corals, and rock. Later the CO banned this activity as being too dangerous and certainly not appropriate in front of the Officers and Sergeants Mess.

The 16th of November 1966 was one of the more memorable celebrations. It was Peter Suna's birthday and the night kicked off in the Sergeant's Mess with Lt General Thomas Daley, Chief of General Staff of the Australian Army, appearing in the Sgts Mess and offering his congratulations. From there the evening deteriorated. At a certain point in the evening one of Peter's so-called mates devised a lethal chug-a-lug cocktail. Pete was found some time later, on the beach, unconscious. His mates then procured his bed from his donga and laid him out to recover right there on the beach. Some fifty years on, despite the list of culprits being well known, Peter is still searching for the mastermind of these pranks.

So, with regular dining-in nights, movies, sport, cards and darts and, trips to town and basketball and AFL competitions, and an occasional invitation cricket or rugby match against visiting Royal Australian Navy ships, the two years away from home seemed to be passing quickly.

39. Max inspecting a Japanese WWII memorial near Matupi Volcano, during a trip to an AFL carnival at Rabaul in 1967.

CHAPTER TWELVE

A SPORTING LIFE

Moem Barracks had just opened and in 1966 it had no recreational facilities, cafes, theatres, or sporting facilities except for a squash court, obviously included in the master plan for use by Australian Officers and NCOs. The expansion of the TPNG Army had brought together the diverse and often troublesome tribal system of the country, so sport to some extent could be argued to be a healthy, multicultural, beneficial and unifying activity, and of course, sport served to cement important friendships and serve a purpose beyond the game itself.

Max started as a Chalkie at Moem but then served for a month as temporary 2IC for his allocated infantry Company when a Captain was sent on sick leave back to Australia. As a Sergeant he could not get higher duties pay as an officer. Then he was seconded and became the Regimental Sports Officer, organizing athletics, volleyball, soccer, softball, basketball, and football and staying well away from chalk, blackboards, and classrooms. The sports squad consisted of Max (acting in a Captain's role), a Corporal and a work squad of six soldiers. His main achievements were introducing softball and volleyball competitions, a four-team Wewak Aussie Rules competition, converting the Moem tennis courts into a floodlit basketball court and transforming a swampy patch of kunai grass into a makeshift soccer pitch and athletics track for an intercompany sports day. The intercompany athletics day was a great success despite Max dropping a container of lime (for marking lanes) and burning his face and left eye. Setting up a gymnasium in the new buildings was an additional task and to make a clean break with Education, Max moved into an office at the Gym. The Gym was first class with panelled walls, wooden floors, showers, offices, and a new squash court.

The sporting programs at the camp included 'civvy' basketball teams from outside the camp, alongside men's and women's teams formed from enlisted personnel and their families. The women's games at night became popular, attracting crowds of 200 or more. This was not surprising as the women's team from the Hospital were all young nurses, and of course 2PIR had a thousand mostly single young soldiers trapped on the base. The popularity of basketball led to the opening of a new floodlight basketball court in Wewak town, opened by the District Commissioner. PIR played a demonstration game against a Wewak team after the speeches. Max was also responsible for producing a weekly cyclostyled newsletter for the camp, called "PIR News", used for sporting results and coming events. This was a busy schedule as Max was also Regimental Property Officer (in charge of auditing and distributing all sports gear) and Bar Treasurer of the Sergeants Mess. By September, Max was complaining to his parents that he "had another week of paperwork … Bar stock takes, ledgers, sports inventory, etc. all very necessary and take hours to straighten out and complete".

Squash in the 1960s was then a relatively new sport in Australia. In Perth, Rick recalls that at his school in 1962, a squash court was a part of the campus and teachers and students had many opportunities to play and compete. Rick had proven to be a poor tennis player but took to squash reasonably well and went on to play pennant squash for some years, both before and after Nasho. Moem Barracks had a single squash court sitting alone in an otherwise sparse area. Weird! It was in poor shape, but it served its purpose even though it was not used a great deal. A few others played. Rick had become friendly with an Australian Nurse from the Boram hospital, Fay, who played very well, and they enjoyed many competitive games. Rick thought he was pretty good at squash, but he often was brought back to earth. On Rick's return to TPNG as a civilian in 1970, his boss was Geoff Ord, aged 51 compared to Rick's 24 years. Rick mentioned to Geoff that he enjoyed squash and was invited for a game at Moresby's un-air-conditioned squash centre. Rick admits he was taken apart at the seams. When the torture ended Rick asked Geoff Ord if he played competitively, giving him an opportunity to mention that he had been a TPNG National Champion. Thanks!

Max in his new role as Regimental Sports Officer organized for goalposts to appear and both basketball and Aussie Rules (AFL) competitions started with Army and civilian teams quickly joining in the fun. This was all due to Max's persuasive proposals put to the camp CO, who enthusiastically endorsed all this sport as conducive to improved Battalion fitness, harmony, and Army-town relations. Sport was playing a positive role in 2PIR's morale and fitness.

The basketball at Moem was played at nights under lights and provided exercise, socialisation, and fun. The games were taken seriously but played mainly for enjoyment. Max's lust for goals continued with his irresistible habit of attempting outside jump shots on every possible opportunity. Laurie's fingers were again prominent in contests for loose balls. TPNG colleagues and friends also took more readily to this game, as many had played previously. Imaginatively, the intrepid six named themselves the "Education Sergeants". Rick was the gun player; Max hogged the shooting and Pete, and Laurie were the two tall guards. Bob made up the numbers. In the 1967 Grand Final, the "Education Sergeants" were up against a team of NCOs from Buka Island, an impressive team of tall, very black-skinned athletes. They had named themselves the "Buka Sergeants". At the end, the scoreboard showed a draw. Then in dramatic fashion it was revealed an error had been made and the "Education Sergeants" had won by a point. What a fiasco.

Most of the Nasho Six, as young men, had considerable interest in sport although backgrounds and tastes varied. Max from Victoria and Laurie, Bob and Rick from WA had grown up with and enjoyed AFL. Peter started with rugby but was a hidden talent who later found he was able to excel at almost every sporting endeavour from triathlons to golf. He largely kept his talents under a bush at Wewak.

Expanding the Wewak AFL football competition to four teams in 1967, was a significant event and there was no shortage of willing participants from both local and expatriate soldiers of all ranks. The new Moem team, imaginatively named "Army", could well be argued to have been a truly uniting and multicultural team. The Six Chalkies were prominent with Laurie

"Fingers" Bowman at Full-Back saving many a goal on the tips of his constantly mangled fingers; centre half-back Max was always seeking to kick a goal from the other side of the centre line; half-back Mason with head down and backside up was disturbing any pack he could locate; and "Rooster" Rick Larsen vainly sought glory in the centre as Max's dropkicks soared over his head into the forward line. Football was fun, bringing pleasure not only to the Army team but to the other three civvy teams – Wirui Catholic Mission, Town, and Brandi High School, the last comprised of secondary school students and a couple of teachers. It was hardly an even competition with a fit adult Army team, a team of adolescent schoolboys and Mission and Town teams of various degrees of expat and local experience, skill and fitness. The Grand Final in 1967 was played in front of 2000 locals (Wewak's population was around 9000). The 2PIR Pipe band entertained the crowd at half-time and the 2PIR CO presented the Winning Shield. The District Commissioner presented the League Best and Fairest Award, won by John Harangau, a tenacious long-kicking rover and young gun player from Brandi High School. A mate from the Mess, Sgt Carl Waldhauser was the umpire and donated the cup for the winning team. WO "Wriggles" Wriggley was a goal umpire. Padre Clift acted as team manager and his two teenage sons both played for PIR. The Army team had gone through the season undefeated and won the 1967 Grand Final by six goals, but that was not the point. Army later beat a combined team made up of the other three teams in a special match as a demonstration of the fun to be had playing footy. In a piece on Wewak's AFL competition that Max published in the 1967 Queensland AFL's Annual Report, he stated that in the next year "the same four teams will be certain starters and possibly another Army team and another from Brandi (High School) can be included. (Wewak's) small population and its wide distribution limit us, but footy is here to stay for sure". 2PIR entered two teams in the Wewak AFL competition in 1968, imaginatively named "Red" and Green", 2PIR's Battalion colours.

In 1968, Sgt Peter Anasis wrote to Max saying the basketball and sport competitions at 2PIR and Wewak were struggling and needed someone to act as coordinator. Max acknowledges this was his error in not ensuring there was a succession plan in place, an error he tried hard to avoid in subsequent projects and initiatives he was involved in across the Pacific Islands, but which he also acknowledges he was mostly unsuccessful in achieving. AFL struggled along but by 2000, the senior and schools' competitions at Wewak had collapsed.

Staff Sergeant Bob Wriggley loved AFL. Bob was brilliant! He was the regular goal umpire and masseur but also took on the role of passing the port, as in alcohol, at quarter time breaks. Not everyone participated but maybe this could be called the "X" factor. Wriggley Bob (as he was often called) wrote programs, gave out nicknames and meant as much to AFL at Wewak as any player on the ground. Bob was also a committed, obsessive St Kilda fan and Darrel Baldock was his football God. So much so that one night Bob ran into the Sgt's mess, in full St Kilda regalia, and stab-passed a kick from the doorway to the bar – behind which stood wide-eyed bar manager, National Serviceman Laurence Bowman. Characters such as the Padre, Carl Waldhauser and Bob Wriggley really deserve a special mention and not just for "Wriggles" goal umpiring and his AFL footy column signed "Around the Ground with Darrel Baldock". Bob was a great mate and a link between the Nasho Six and the Regs. Thanks Wriggles!

In June 1967, a representative Wewak AFL team went by air to Madang for an inter-town game thanks to Max organising a free flight courtesy of Ansett-MAL. Wewak had a strong team which now included the Army Doctor, Ian Hill, who went on to play league football in WA and a newly arrived Chalkie Nasho, Kerry Dohring, who later played for Sturt in SA. The ground at Madang was interesting as there was a telephone pole wrapped in mattresses on the wing, perhaps 40 metres from the centre circle. The game was of a remarkably high standard, a great spectacle, attracted a sizable local crowd, and attracted reports in the two TPNG daily newspapers.

Army regulations required 2PIR players off-base to wear long trousers, long-sleeved white shirts and ties during the evening, a malaria precaution.

The Madang League were rather disorganised and little effort was made to provide social activities for the visitors from Wewak.

As they were spending two nights in Madang a group of seven smartly attired Australians and Papua New Guineans, went to the Madang Club. They were refused entry and when Rick asked why he was told the group was inappropriately dressed. They stood there for a while wondering what to do. Peter Mamare, then a CSM, from Buka, told Rick not to bother being refused entry as it was treatment he had experienced before. This little scene made it quite clear that discrimination based on race was prevalent in Madang in the 1960s.

This was a great shock to the Nasho Six, sheltered inside Moem camp from this type of racist attitude. (The Madang Club is now open and inclusive and Peter Mamare's son, Fabian, reports he often has a few beers there!)

40. The Port Moresby Post-Courier report on the Madang-Wewak game in 1967. Max as Wewak's Coach thanking the losing opposition.

The Nasho Six are still troubled by collective, generalist, racist views as throughout their subsequent careers they worked in Indigenous communities in Australia and the Pacific Islands and always enjoyed the tolerance and inclusiveness, sadly not found in Madang.

There was a Territory-wide inter-league competition held in Rabaul in 1967 which the Wewak competition could not afford to send a team to, but somehow Max acquired complimentary air tickets for himself and Rick, travelling overnight via Lae where they over-nighted at PIR's Igam Barracks - with countless frogs – a tale for another day. After being off-loaded due to their free tickets, they were stranded in Lae for two days and finally got to Rabaul late on Sunday afternoon, in time only to watch a match on Monday and attend an Inter-territory AFL meeting. There was discussion of a Papua versus New Guinea Aussie Rules game to be played in either Mt Hagen or Goroka, as a kind of middle ground. Due to the logistics and the expense, this game never took place during the Nasho Six's time in TPNG. The Port Moresby competition was strong with a number of ex-VFL players, but Max reported to his parents that a Wewak side "could easily beat Rabaul and Lae ... the game is certain to go ahead in the Territory".

The CO at Moem Barracks, Col Donald Ramsay, saw AFL and indeed all sports as an excellent medium for community relations as well as diverting the attention of soldiers in camp towards fitness gained through competitive team building and sporting activities. The evening basketball competitions, football, cricket, surfing, and squash provided exercise, socialisation, and fun, played with serious intent but mainly for enjoyment.

41. Cover of the Pamphlet prepared by Bob Wriggley for the Wewak AFL Grand Final 1967.

Over the duration of the Nasho Chalkie program in TPNG from 1966 to 1973, several Chalkies coached AFL teams at Wewak and Port Moresby, and played in TPNG representative squash, soccer, and rugby teams.

Max's letter home to his parents recorded a typical day in their sporting life at Moem Barracks (6 Feb 1967), "After work Pete, John and I went to Battalion training for the rugby league team ... should get a game in a team as there are two teams .... After training we had a game of basketball and then a swim. After tea, Rick and I went and played squash for an hour and a half ... so I am certainly getting plenty of exercise".

42. Wewak peninsula, 1966. The swamps in the foreground have now been filled in. The main street still runs from left to right along the base of the hill.

CHAPTER THIRTEEN

WEWAK: GOING TO TOWN

The Army camp at Moem was eighteen kilometres from Wewak town along a gravel road with only the aerodrome, the Public Hospital on Boram point and the Catholic Mission compound in between. Wewak, a centre for the local TPNG administration, was more like a shanty town or frontier town far removed from the modern world. Even though it was a port, the jetties only catered for small local boats and coastal traders. Large freighters had to anchor offshore and load and unload using lighters. The main and only street nestled under Wewak Hill, a promontory or large tombola that jutted out into the Admiralty Sea linked to the mainland by flat swampy land. A street of 100 metres ran from the beach on the west across the base of the promontory to the jetties on the eastern shore. Scattered along the shore were a petrol station, depots, distribution centres, a construction company, and a few offices. A hotel, the Wewak Club, government offices and numerous living quarters were on top of the peninsula, known as Wewak Hill. The Hotel seemed inviting at first, but it was soon discovered the beer was many times dearer than at the subsidised Sergeants Mess Bar, and after seeing the sign that read

"No Dogs. No Natives", it was never visited by the Nasho Six. The European population of government and port officials numbered a dozen with a slightly larger Chinese community running trade stores and other businesses. Indigenous villages were spread along the coast and inland, but Wewak never seemed to be densely populated at least when viewed from the coast road. Later, when there were no waves at Ferok, Max and his surfing mates took a tour by truck around back roads and tracks and discovered to their surprise, thickly populated villages, which immediately changed their opinion about the Wewak region being sparsely populated.

Going to Wewak on Saturday mornings meant a road trip in an army vehicle, on motor bikes or in Rick's "Little Red Renault". On the roadside, local Sepik people sat selling local vegetables and fruit. It was common for these vendors and others idling about nearby to be chewing 'betel', thinly sliced betel nut mixed with slaked lime, and to spit it out on the ground or a nearby wall, leaving large red stains everywhere. Frequent betel nut users were easy to identify because of the red staining, and permanent cancerous damage it caused to the mouth, lips, and teeth. The attraction of the nut, apart from it being free, was that it stimulated the central nervous system and could bring about mild euphoria. It is addictive along the same vein as caffeine or tobacco and certainly does not add to personal appearance. It was banned in the Army even though betel nut chewing was regarded by some as having traditional cultural importance.

Rick recalls the clustered sameness of the Chinese shops and the walls and footpaths with betel nut splattered everywhere and smiles of red-stained teeth. He also recalls a guy outside the Wewak Hotel who sold actual baby crocodiles, known as puk-

puks. Tourists often bought carved wooden crocodiles, stained black, but the Wewak Hotel versions were alive, and their teeth were sharp. They were not huge but when pulled out of a hessian bag it was appropriate to watch your fingers. Puk-puks were quite common along the north coast and rivers and in Madang, for example, signs were displayed advising potential bathers of the presence of crocodiles.

As there was not much to do in Wewak, being out of bounds most of the time did not really matter to the ordinary soldiers. The rule at Moem Barracks that ORs were not allowed to go into Wewak town was probably instigated to prevent tribal brawling, drunkenness, or disturbances over access to women. On some Saturdays, a large Army 3-ton truck would take fifty soldiers on "approved leave" into town and the Nasho Six also took this option, until the arrival of Rick's little red Renault or the new Mopeds.

The hospital, halfway to town, was also out of bounds much to the Nasho Six's disappointment, although this rule was regularly ignored. Most of the Australian nurses were older but the Nasho Six socialized if they could sneakily arrange a visit. Rick recalls a particularly raucous party when the then 2PIR Doctor was reclining all over a three-seat sofa with his belly protruding conspicuously. Simultaneously, and with limited dexterity, he thought it would appeal to the female audience to pour two stubbies of South Pacific Lager at once into his gaping mouth. This tactic was not followed by his successor, West Australian Dr Ian Hill, (who became a key player in the 2PIR AFL team) or by any of the Nasho

Six. On one occasion Max reported to his parents that he "went into town yesterday and was lucky enough to get a double-headed ice-cream, a beaut treat". Max made it clear to his parents that living on the base was preferable to being in town; writing home that "actually the base is a town of its own and has all the conveniences of any large modern Victorian town. Can't say the same for Wewak though".

43. Peter with a WWII Japanese landing barge, at the eastern end of the main street; Wewak 1966.

Wewak's isolation on the north coast was partially broken by a gravel road that ran inland to Maprik in the Torricelli Range.

You could also go a few kilometres east along the coast to Brandi High School and about the same distance west past Wewak for a few kilometres to Wom Point, where an obelisk marked the site of the Japanese surrender in New Guinea. (A more impressive memorial is now located there). That was it. So, the Nasho Six stayed mostly at Moem Barracks. This meant the two years were mostly spent inside the camp.

This was not a problem as the camp had squash and basketball courts, a bar and dining facilities, movie nights, and a private beach right in the front of the Sergeants Mess *sak-sak* dongas. The new Mopeds were not good on hills or gravel, so they were used mostly for hooning around the camp roads.

Getting away from Wewak was limited. Apart from AFL footy trips to Madang and Rabaul, the off-base activities by the Nasho Six were a posting to Vanimo (a much sought-after privilege), or a training bivouac at the PNGVR camp in the Highlands near Mt Hagen. Patrolling with infantry platoons along the border provided another escape. Pete and Max also took a short holiday at Christmas to Rabaul.

One trip to town involved Max on Orderly Sergeant Duty taking a squad into town to prevent a brawl occurring when locals alleged a soldier on leave was inappropriately talking to a local girl. Amid shouting and gesturing, it turned out the girl was the soldier's sister, and a potential incident was settled amicably. Other activities off-base involved acting as Marshalls at a Brandi Boys High School sports day and a Sunday spent building a new classroom at the local Wewak Primary school. There were segregated A Primary and T Primary schools. The A schools followed an Australian curriculum, and the T followed a special curriculum for Indigenous children. Each day, 174 children went from the base into town to attend these schools, until mid-1967 when a Primary school was opened on the base. There was also a girls-only High School at the Catholic Mission, deliberately sited 30 km away from the boys-only High School because parents made this a condition of sending their daughters away from the village for schooling. Both high schools went to Form 4 and used the NSW curriculum. Parents paid a $2 annual fee for schooling. Max wrote home that, "kids get education, board, two sets of clothing and all the books etc. for nothing. It costs the Administration quite a deal, but it will pay off in a better future for the country".

Because Max's dad was involved in Rotary back in Colac, Victoria, Max arranged a swap of banners between the Wewak and Colac Clubs and attended a meeting of Wewak Rotary at the "Country Club" (Bowls and Golf Club). The meeting discussed community projects such as tanks and showers in all villages around Wewak and the establishment of a duck farm in a nearby village to provide income and livelihoods. There was an Agricultural Department demonstration farm located behind Wewak airport. Beginning in 1969, a Nasho *Didiman* was posted to 2PIR to develop farming strategies on the base for soldiers preparing to return to their villages after leaving the army.

The golf course in town was regarded to be "top notch" but rarely visited except for occasional events such as a quiz night in the clubhouse. Max reported to his parents that he went to town to play golf (once) and tennis (twice). Max could not recall much about going to town until he read the letters, sent home to his parents in 1966-67. These letters revealed that either singly or as a group, the Nasho Six were regularly in town at the Post Office mailing stuff back home, playing basketball in a local comp, watching the local three-team AFL competition (expanded in 1967 to four teams), attending parties at the Nurses Quarters at Boram Hospital, going to movies in town, attending a Mannequin Parade, a fund-raising dance at the Wewak Club and the Presidents Ball at the "Sepik Club", visiting the Rotary Club and shopping for bargains, especially electrical goods, watches and cameras. Max mostly remembered marching about the base in starched greens and pursuing other military matters, and riding his Moped here and there, but until he read his letters home to his parents, rediscovered in a box in 2018, he had not realised how much time he had spent off the base. The arrival of Rick's Renault and the subsequent purchase of motorbikes and Mopeds had facilitated all this zooming in and out of town and Max in his role as Sports Officer also meet local 'expats', (colloquialism for expatriates, or Europeans), Chinese and other civvies and struck up friendships outside of camp.

In 2017, Peter visited Wewak on a P&O cruise and was given a guided tour of the camp by the Camp Commandant who expressed disappointment that the Army has little archival material of the opening of the camp and the Nasho Chalkie period. Max also visited on a P&O cruise in 2018 and was surprised to see that Wewak town had not changed much in the previous fifty years. The single street of shops, rusting hulks along the shore, and a straggling collection of new and old buildings along the shore of the bay seemed not to have changed. One noticeable change was that artefact sellers were coming to town to meet cruise ships, travelling over the Prince Alexandra range from the distant Sepik River basin. Wewak is now one of six districts that make up Papua New Guinea's East Sepik Province, with a population of

20,000. The surrounding district has over 100,000. Wewak is now PNG's eleventh largest urban area.

44. ANSETT-MAL flight into Telefomin. The flight path out was through the cloud-shrouded mountains.

CHAPTER FOURTEEN

SEARCHING FOR MISSING PLANES

John and Bob were doing an Education posting at the Vanimo outpost, normally a relaxing and rather cushy posting, but one evening the Company commander, Major Graeme Manning, came into the combined Officers and Sergeant's Mess looking grim, and everyone responded formally – disturbing Vanimo's generally relaxed atmosphere. The CO looked worried. "OK men, a Mission plane has gone missing near Telefomin and the Army is sending in an aircraft to assist with the search. I will be in charge. I want two volunteers as observers". The Mess went quiet. You could hear a pin drop. "Thanks, men, for volunteering," he said pointing at Sgts Sweeney and Mason, "I will pick you up at first light". So began the search for a missing Mission plane.

After a specially prepared early breakfast at 5am, Bob and John, equipped with pack and bedroll, were met by Major Manning. The Cessna left Vanimo at first light and landed two hours later at the remote mountain strip at Telefomin, an

Administration patrol post tucked away high in the central cordillera or massive central mountain range, near the Indonesian border. This was regarded by all as the most remote outpost of the Australian administration in TPNG.

During the day, several planes made sweeps over the expected crash area without luck. There was probably a dozen or more aircraft involved in the search, checking each sector in a very systematic grid pattern. Due to refuelling and constant discussions and monitoring of the area being searched, Bob and John often had an hour to fill in between flights. On one layover, an ex-pat pilot produced a cricket bat and ball – not sure where from - but a game of tip and run cricket was soon being played on the edge of the grass airport runway. There were a dozen players and great fun was had by all. Some New Guineans in red lap-laps cutting grass at the edge of the tarmac saw the game of cricket so they dropped their metal scythes and scampered over to join in, but not for long. A police officer ran to where the game was being played, loudly blowing his police whistle, and shouted at the New Guineans. The men, prisoners, immediately left the field of play and jogged back to where their scythes had been dropped and continued cutting grass just like nothing had happened. We found out later that these eight men, all accused of murder, were on supervised work release from the local jail. They had attacked a neighbouring village while most of its men were away hunting and several villagers were killed. Bob and John were surprised because the chaps in red lap laps seemed cheerful and friendly. Of all the new and amazing adventures in their time as Education Sergeants in New Guinea, that friendly game of cricket, with murderers, would take the cake as the least expected way to spend spare time deep in the mountains.

Towards late afternoon the search party was rounded up and it was announced that the search aircraft had to leave Telefomin as monsoon storms were forecast for the surrounding ranges. The pilots assured everyone the flights out would be OK. Wrong! The storm swept in and the little Cessna could not make the high altitude needed to go over the top of the mountain range. A decision was made, an ominous one it seemed to Sergeants Mason and Sweeney. The pilot was told to take off but stay low in the winding valleys until the Sepik River plains could be reached and a safe route plotted north over the Torricelli Mountain range to Vanimo. In a rather unconvincing manner, possibly said for his own benefit, Major Manning stated, "OK men, no need to worry, we'll be fine".

The Cessna took off and there were simple instructions – "Mason you look left and if you see cliffs, precipices or ridges, shout cliffs left" and approximately how far. Sweeney you do the same on the right side, but yell "cliffs right". With a massive storm billowing above and surrounded by a jumble of deep valleys and ridgelines, the Cessna began weaving its way down narrow twisting valleys with John and Bob glued to the little Cessna's windows. This flight was an aviation masterpiece. Captain Manning used a map, compass and watch balanced on his knees to quickly calculate measurements against airspeed, direction, and distance before giving the pilot instructions to turn left or right down a particular valley or along a ridge line. The pilot was glued to his instruments and veered left or right according to the CO's shouted instructions. For an hour, trapped in a noisy, cramped cabin, surrounded by land rushing by close on all sides, Bob and John sweated, stuck to their task, and probably prayed. John recalls that it was truly frightening. Eventually through a break in the cloud the shining waters of the Sepik River gorge could be seen far below as it snaked its way towards the Sepik plains. Then whoosh, out into the sunshine and they were flying sedately over a massive jungle-clad, drainage basin system that meanders a thousand kilometres to the sea on the north coast of New Guinea. Up over the low coastal ranges of the Torricelli Mountains and they were back at Vanimo. Mason and Sweeney were ordered to wait by the waiting Land Rover while the pilot received a rocket, probably for agreeing to go up to Telefomin without checking on the weather forecasts. In a much more relaxed manner, the two Sergeants and the CO headed off in the vehicle while the pilot was left to his own contemplations. The good news was the CO's next order - "Meet me in the Mess, my shout and I am ordering a stand-down day for you both tomorrow". So, a welcome shower and change of clothes, as well as the promise of a day off on stand-down, ended this little adventure in the mountains of TPNG.

Flying, the Nasho Six had already discovered, was very much by the seat of the pants in those days and STOL (Short Take-off and Landing) was an acronym everyone knew. Some of the remote airstrips were really only a flattened ridge top and pilots had to either drop off the end of the strip into a valley below or ascend quickly and then turn hard to avoid a sheer cliff virtually at the end of the strip. Navigation was visual using prominent landmarks to judge distance from and direction to and from strips. There were few beacons and no GPS, so pilots carefully remembered routes from previous flights. The Japanese and Americans had built twenty or so airstrips during the Pacific War and postwar these had become the aerodromes servicing the major coastal towns. In the absence of roads across most of the Territory, the

Cessna, STOL and reconfigured DC3s were the lifeline linking New Guinea's peoples with the modern world. Mission Aviation Fellowship (MAF) was an airline in all respects and Mission pilots were already a legend by this time. Jim Sinclair, *Balus - the Aeroplane in Papua New Guinea* (1990) is an excellent three volume history of commercial aviation in New Guinea, and highly recommended. (Volume I: *The Early Years*, Volume II: *The Rise of Talair*, Volume III: *Wings of a Nation*)

Air supremacy had proved to be a deciding factor in the Pacific War, not only offensively, but for reconnaissance and resupply and while the Pacific War cemented the strategic importance of air transport in wartime, it also led directly to the expansion of air services for commerce, passenger, and freight in TPNG in the 1950s and 1960s. As Nashos plucked from both farming communities and the suburbs it was an eye-opener to be in and out of commercial flights on the converted DC-3's and the newer DC4 of Ansett-MAL, as well as in Bell, Iroquois and Chinook helicopters, Caribou, the giant Hercules transport plane, and the much-loved Cessna. The Fokker and the Boeing 727 were the next generation. In a letter home Max reported he had also flown in a "twin-engine, ten-seater Piaggi ... much better than the DC-3. The Fokker Friendships and Boeing 727 services have started so those will just about seal the fate of the old DC-3". (This prediction proved to be accurate.)

It was always a thrill to take a 'swan' on a Caribou from Wewak up to Vanimo along the Aitape coast, with the loading ramp down, skimming the waves looking for crocodiles as the Caribou zoomed over Japanese-built airstrips littered with bomb craters, from just twenty years earlier, and finally drop down on Vanimo's strip with the bay at one end and the ocean at the other.

On a P&O cruise in 2017, Max met a former Army Caribou pilot who remembered a trip to Vanimo in 1967 with Nashos hanging out the back taking photographs. He had been the pilot.

The wreckage of the missing Mission aircraft Bob and John unsuccessfully tried to find in 1966 was found forty years later in 2006.

CHAPTER FIFTEEN

RADIO BLONG YUMI

In 1966, transistor radios were cheap and easily accessible in Wewak's Chinese trade stores. The Nasho Six could switch on each day to Radio Australia being re-broadcast into the Territory of Papua New Guinea. However, it was not Radio Australia that they tuned into at nights at Moem, but *Radio Blong Yumi*, the local radio station more commonly known as *Radio Red Wing* after its radical young firebrand announcer Michael Somare. Later to become the first and a long-standing PM of the new nation after 1975, (He died in 2021) Somare had been banished to the provinces for being too outspoken in Port Moresby, and then after making similar commentary on Australian rule in the Territory at Wewak, he was dragged back to Moresby so he could be better watched and supervised.

Meanwhile, the Nasho Six bopped along to a nightly barrage of country and western music, clearly the most popular music among the local Sepik population. Mostly this was presented in *tok pisin*, so the Nasho Six had only a rough idea what was being said, but Johnny Cash (*Ring of Fire*), Roger Miller (*King of the Road*) and others like Glen Campbell, Johnny Horton, Tammy

Wynette, Patsy Cline and Marty Robbins, were universal. So as soon as they heard, "*Taim I kam up long 9 kilok*" (It is 9 o'clock!) you knew there was a solid session of country and western about to fill the airwaves.

Local bands recorded *tok pisin* versions of the big overseas songs on cassettes, along with a growing repertoire of New Guinea material. The cassette music industry was widespread in all towns in TPNG, and little studios were pumping out a remarkable array of local and imported songs. The Nasho favourite in 1966 was a number called "*Tupela meri I wasim sak sak*" (Two women washing sago in preparation for cooking). In a two-year posting to Moem Barracks, this was heard many times every week. *Radio blong Yumi* also had regular news broadcasts, often acting as a voice for the Australian administration, and covered some local issues and events. This was all presented in *tok pisin*.

Radio had a fascinating history in Papua New Guinea, with many national and local stations broadcasting in AM, FM, and shortwave. Radio provided the main access and communication between the government and the people of the TPNG, separated by long distances with either no roads or at best rough tracks, and in 1966-1967 with no television or access to the daily newspapers published in Lae, Rabaul and Port Moresby. Today, near the 2PIR outpost of Vanimo, Radio Gabriel operates on shortwave into nearby West Papua across the Indonesian border, one of twenty locally operated shortwave stations across the nation. Port Moresby now has 26 radio stations.

Radio reception direct from Australia was possible in certain parts of TPNG in the 1960s if you had the correct equipment. Wewak was too remote to allow for easy shortwave access. Rick took listening to a higher level when he returned to live in Lae in

1970. Whenever the opportunity arose, he would sit in a deck chair in the back yard with a short-wave radio, with a wire aerial stretching up and around the house's water tank. Then, patiently, he would search for ABC Radio Perth and listen to a broadcast of live Western Australian Football League straight from home!

This was the era in which membership of the Australian Record Club was nearly compulsory and albums were delivered in the mail promptly, ordered from the ARC catalogue. Max had a selection of LPs and was often writing to his parents, who were also ARC members, advising them which LPs to order from the ARC catalogue, such as *Good Vibrations* (The Beach Boys), Frankie Lane's "*Hell Bent for Leather*" and the Everley Brothers "*Golden hits*". Rick focussed on Nancy Sinatra's *These boots are made for walking*, Peter, Paul and Mary and Simon and Garfunkel and what he called "other refined music". Other Nasho favourites were *Paint it black* (The Rolling Stones), *Hitchhiker* (Bobbie and Laurie) and *Friday on my mind* (The Easybeats). When writing up his part of this story and checking letters home to his parents, Max found a recommendation to his parents to buy "*Swinging Safari*" by Bert Kaempfert, a big band star, and coincidentally the inspiration in 2018 for a nostalgic Australian comedy film of the same name, set in the 1960s.

In TPNG and deep in Sepik Province, the Nasho Six were vaguely aware of the top ten songs in Australia in 1966-1967, but as *Radio blong Yumi* reminded them each and every night, there were really only two popular types of music in the Territory, Country AND Western. What a pleasant way it was to end the day.

45. The "little Red Renault", 1968.

46. Rick with his Little Red Renault, 1967 (Sgt Carl Waldhauser's VW in background).

CHAPTER SIXTEEN

LITTLE RED RENAULT and a NIGHT TO REMEMBER

Social life improved when Rick had his little red Renault 750 shipped up from Australia at Army expense. In Rick's second year of study at Teachers' College in 1964, he had bought his first car for 100 pounds (two years before decimal currency) – a blue 1952 Renault 750, or 4CV, a model that had been used as both a police car and taxi in France. It was an absolute gem and gave no trouble. The choice was made because Rick had a school friend with a similar car in Year 12. It was economical and roomy enough, although tiny. Advertisements advised potential buyers to be wary of the loss of power when travelling uphill. The 4CV super-charged rear engine often went on to a second life in industrial-level lawnmowers. After graduating from Teachers' College in 1964, Rick left WA for the first time, travelling by train – which was then cheaper than flying – to Melbourne.

He only had enough money for a one-way ticket with a few quid to spare until he found a temporary job. Rick had to be back in

WA for the start of the 1965 school year and his first teaching appointment. On arrival in Victoria, he went to book a return ticket, hoping to pay later, but this was not allowed. So, with a touch of real sadness, he sent his Dad a telegram asking him to sell his blue 4CV – which his Dad soon did for 75 quid ($150.00).

When the Army posted Rick to 1BOD Ordnance Corps in Brisbane, and he thought it would be for the duration of his Nasho service, Rick figured another Renault was in order – this time a red 1954 model – and a dud! Rick's mechanical skills were poor as he was better equipped to deal with Latin, English, and Maths. Then came the posting to Wewak and, for reasons still unclear, the Army was prepared to ship the car to Wewak for Rick at Army expense.

It was an offer too good to refuse. Soon after his arrival in Wewak, Rick was informed the car was on the wharf in Port Moresby and could travel no further until it underwent quarantine and cleaning. The threat was a charge of $50 a day if the car was on that wharf for more than seven days. Help! A couple of Nasho Education Corps Chalkies Rick had met on arrival in Port Moresby came to the fore – Rick does not recall their names – and they voluntarily did whatever cleaning was required and soon it was ship-bound for northern shores.

Rick was the only Nasho at Moem with a car, so negotiations ensued, and five new co-owners handed over the princely sum of $15 each on the understanding that all were now equal owners of what was possibly the smallest car in TPNG.

There were hardly any tar-sealed sections of road in Wewak at the time and the roads inland to Maprik or east and west along the coast were gravel or crushed coral. Amazingly the tyres survived many journeys on the rough road to and from town but were soon worn down to the canvas underlay. With no steel linings in those days, the tyres must have known every sharp crack and rock along the road. If ever a Renault deserved an Endurance Medal it was Little Red. The Renault endured thanks to Laurie's skills as a mechanic extraordinaire, and along the way created many unforgettable memories.

The accelerator cable broke and was replaced by fishing line from the rear engine to the driver's side quarter-window which then became the default accelerator. The fly window, described in the manual as the air-conditioning system, thus became the accelerator and led to a new set of driving skills required when changing gears (that were non-synchronised). Driving the Renault required the deft manipulation of the driver's side fly window while keeping the other hand on the steering wheel. The clutch also died and so push-starts became the order of the day, timed with quarter-window accelerator manoeuvres. On one occasion Laurie was working to fix the clutch and became a tad frustrated so he ordered everyone to tip the little Renault over on its roof so he could work on the chassis more easily. At some point in the clutch saga, a spare part was needed and amazingly it was obtained from Rabaul, far away on New Britain Island.

The Renault offered a lifestyle; trips to town, stop-offs at the Nurses' Quarters – where it was a source of amusement rather than a 'chick magnet'. Somehow, six fully grown guys could fit in, if somewhat awkwardly. Coming down Wewak Hill was always one of the more serious tests for Le Renault. On one occasion at night, Rick was at the wheel in full quarter-window accelerator coordination mode. A push start got the Renault heading downhill rather quickly and in the cramped jumble of bodies and limbs, Rick fumbled for the headlight switch and found it just in time to avoid the cyclone fence surrounding a storage yard at the bottom of the hill.

On another evening when arriving back at the barracks, the Little Red Renault was greeted by the soldier on duty at the Moem boom gates with the inevitable, "Halt! Who goes there?" Max responded "Mickey Mouse". Nonplussed the soldier stated, "You not him. I saw him before" and then waved the Renault through.

The most memorable or infamous, incident involving the Little Red Renault began when the Education Sergeants were challenged to a game of darts by a team of "civvies" from the Hotel in Wewak town. Darts had become a major evening pastime for the Education Sergeants, often to the chagrin of the "Regs", and eventually a shared use of the Mess's solitary and heavily pummelled dart board was sorted out. The invitation from Town was accepted and an Education Corps team chosen comprising Pete, Laurie, Bob, and Max. They drove the Little Red Renault into town in the dark on an otherwise quiet Friday night. On the way to town the alternator light started flashing which meant if the headlights were left on the battery would soon expire. It was decided that the trip to town should be made without lights.

Luckily, traffic on Wewak's coast road was normally light, and on a Friday night virtually non-existent. Traffic police had yet to be introduced into TPNG. Pete was driving and managed to miss a turn in the dark and the Renault headed ingloriously into the bush and was bogged. With a suitable barrage of cursing and ridicule, the Renault was pushed back on the road.

At the tavern, the Renault was parked facing downhill so it could be easily started. The darts were noisy and competitive but the "wanna-be" champions from the Sergeants Mess were soundly beaten. Several rounds of drinks were probably the cause for some mis-directed killer shots. The team then headed home and Bob, despite his father's advice never to volunteer, decided to be the driver. A quick push to start, and with no lights the Renault headed downhill and out of town. Approaching the camp, Bob decided to avoid entering through the main gate as a darkened Renault full of tipsy Sergeants would have attracted unwanted attention. Bob decided to take the back road and enter the camp through a new tar-sealed road via the LEP married quarters. There were no streetlights. In the dark without headlights, the Renault crashed through a bamboo barrier put up to keep cars off the road until streetlights were installed. Too late!! The bamboo barrier splintered into small pieces. Bob made a snap decision and decided to just keep driving and headed through the camp back to the Sergeants Mess. Bob was a little casual about the consequences or damage to car, or to the barrier, as he knew he was disappearing to Vanimo early in the morning.

The next day the dreaded RSM, Daryl Howells, was told about the smashed barrier, tyre marks and a little red Renault with suspicious marks on its front fenders. All the Education Sergeants were ordered out of bed and sent to cut new bamboo poles, strip away the leaves and paint the poles red and white, and then restore the road barrier. This was not discussed openly in the Mess and certainly more care was taken afterwards to obey road rules and have the headlights functioning. Amazingly no one copped a Duty Sergeant as punishment. The Renault was unscathed and with a new alternator lived on for another year.

When the time came to return to Australia one serious question was what to do with the Renault. So, it was put up for tender.

There were three offers with the winning bid coming from a couple of desperate young "Reg" officers. The amount, $70, was enough to throw one great farewell party - money well spent.

The little Red Renault was later rumoured to have been unceremoniously driven into the Bismarck Sea in front of the Officer's Mess and abandoned. A "Reg" was then rumoured to have salvaged it and tried to get it working. What a car!! On Rick's return to TPNG in the 1970s, he visited Wewak several times and asked about the Renault's whereabouts, ultimately learning of its new home at the local tip. Rick visited and paid his respects to a rusty Little Red laying on its side, in peace at last.

In 2009, Rick bought a Renault 750 on eBay, named "Fifi". It was blue and fully restored. Rick joined the local Renault Club and, with help, further enhanced the restoration. But Rick had largely forgotten how to drive a car without power steering, power brakes or synchronised gears and his sons found it nigh on impossible so after a couple of years of youthful play, "Fifi" went back to eBay. Even today, although driving a Japanese car, Rick uses a Renault keyring.

CHAPTER SEVENTEEN

LCSWTD

An array of diseases and misfortunes were enough for Max's so-called mates to come up with the clumsy acronym - LCSWTD - longest continuous service with tropical disease.

The new arrivals at Moem soon had persistent skin rashes, particularly in the groin area from wearing military-issue, starched thick denim clothing. Adding to the problem was the fact that the water supply at Moem Barracks was connected to the town main, from a weir that had been built across the Brandi River further down the coast, but the older Sgts Mess *sak-sak* buildings had not been connected, so a well near the beach provided water for showers and washing. It was as salty as the sea itself. Special soaps were issued for use in salty water, but shampoo and lathering became a distant memory. At best a warm morning shower could be obtained, but the skin remained gritty all through the day and seemed susceptible to most tropical fungal attacks. Bob designed a remedy by leaving out buckets of water to fill with the usual nightly rainfall. Bob used this to douse himself after having the standard saltwater shower. Bob reckoned he was sweet-smelling and bulletproof after using this technique.

At the end of 1967, after the Nasho Six had departed, the Sergeants Mess moved into flash new buildings in the centre of the camp, with hot mains-water showers.

An Army always places great emphasis on uniform dress codes, and this was a lesson learnt by all Nashos at day-one of Recruit training. And so, it was at 2PIR, despite the tropical heat and humidity. The day-to-day working uniform had to be crisp and ironed and wash-iron bois were employed, and paid by the NCOs and Officers, to keep uniforms up to the required standard. It was a pity about the starch. So much was used that shorts and shirts could almost stand to attention without a body being inserted. These highly starched shorts were not conducive to air flow. The Army Doctor's best offer was to prescribe the reliable old purple Castellani's Paint to be applied to the affected, and sensitive, area – and it stung! The Doctor also authorised "starch-free shorts" for some for a short period of treatment. Experimentation soon taught the wounded that the best method of applying Castellani was to liberally paint a given area while lying on a bed with a fan on full blast aimed at the affected area, usually the groin region. (No photo is included of this practice). Crotch rot continued to be a problem for some well after the Army days were over.

Gentian Violet, or Castellani's paint was used at the time to treat Tinea, or footrot, a common problem for soldiers in the tropics due to constantly wearing damp or wet socks and sharing showers with a ragged assortment of others in the 'ablutions'. The basic Army treatment for tinea, involving the application of an odourless dry powder, was simple and effective.

Bob and Rick suffered from long bouts of prickly heat caused by wearing over-starched uniforms in hot humid conditions.

When Dr Hill wrote Bob and Rick a "chit" allowing them to wear unstarched uniforms until the allergy cleared, the RSM was not pleased, as he considered this a self-inflicted wound and therefore chargeable. Bob admonished his over-enthusiastic *haus boi* and managed to get the level of starch in his uniforms reduced to a healthy level. Bob also suffered a serious bout of blisters while on patrol at Vanimo wearing a new pair of boots. Rick's worst medical recollections are of tinea, a broken molar which was sorted out by a "temporary" filling at the hospital, which lasted 10 years, and a few sporting sprains. Pete came down with a serious bout of hepatitis while posted to Vanimo and John suffered for many years after Nasho from tinnitus because of ear damage suffered during live firing exercises, while the others regarded themselves as fit and sporty types, and bullet-proof.

Max earned his label – LCSWTD – after a bout in hospital with malaria, a long-running problem with tinea and a wound that became ulcerous after he fell spectacularly off his Moped while riding around the corner in front of the old Education Centre *sak-sak* with a hand-held megaphone in one hand yelling abuse at the other Nasho Chalkies. He hit some loose gravel and went flying. This was hilarious at the time, but a fair bit of skin and leg went astray.

Max's ring-worm problem came about in a strange and initially unexplained manner. Unbeknown to Max when he returned to his donga, as did everyone, for a short midday nap during the relatively liberal 90-minute lunch break, he was unknowingly sharing his bed with a feral cat that his neighbouring Sergeant preferred to call "his pet". The neighbouring Sergeant fed this cat in his donga on a regular basis, but it spent most of the day lying on Max's bed. So, when Max collapsed short-less and shirt-less for a midday nap, his bare skin encountered sheets just laid on by the said cat, which had ringworms. It did not take long for the infection to spread, first from five-centimetre rings on the arms and legs then to large circles of reddened skin on the buttocks and back, and finally to the groin. The treatment required the application with a small brush of Gentian Violet crème on to the infected parts twice a day. This included the delicate operation of holding the penis erect and painting it purple, of course done in absolute secrecy with the door and shutters closed. This meant that for many months, Max was multi-coloured under his uniform. Eventually the treatment took effect and Max was free of the extreme desire to scratch away at the cursed weals made by the ringworm parasites.

One day, Max quietly took hold of the said cat, bundled it into a bag and then took the Army runabout out for a spin beyond the reef and disposed of the feline culprit with no remorse or regret. Readers could probably guess that Max has never had, from that time on, a cat for a pet.

CHAPTER EIGHTEEN

FISHING

An amazing and unforgettable experience at Moem Barracks was the huge fish steaks made from Spanish Mackerel and Trevally caught in the waters offshore and grilled on the BBQ at the *haus win*. A Lakatoi would sail past the base and stop off with magnificent fish for sale. The Sergeant's Mess kitchen staff did the buying. This tasted nothing like the flake (actually shark) that was the mainstay of fish-n-chips back in Australia and because it was presented on a plate in hand-sized pieces about thirty millimetres thick, it was a new and amazing taste sensation.

One day a "Reg", Sgt Pat Creeney, invited Bob, Laurie, and Rick out for a day's fishing. Pat was an Irishman, claimed to be a serious fisherman, and was always ready to regale anyone with tales true and tall of his exploits. The party set off just as the sun was rising. They swished along over glassy seas headed excitedly to a reef about 6km out from Moem Point. Pat assured everyone the fish there were at least a metre in length. On reaching the designated spot in an otherwise empty ocean, the lines were cast and trolled behind the slow moving, flat bottomed runabout. The team settled in for a day's fishing. But not for long!

The outboard spluttered and then stopped. It was out of fuel. The spare tank was also empty. Pat assured the team he had checked the previous night and both tanks were full. In the early morning haste to set off no one had bothered to double-check the fuel. Pat was not flustered at all and said, "Grab an oar and we will use the current to paddle back to Moem". Luckily, there were four paddles. So, off the four set, paddling and stopping now and then to take a drink from the water bottles they had all remembered to bring along. After several hours paddling, the beach at the tip of Moem Point could be seen and Pat suggested taking a short cut through and along inside the fringing reef to take a good hour or two off the time to be paddled.

The problem was how to get through a small gap in the reef that led to the lagoon. After a few minutes looking to the calm waters inshore and checking the frequency of some rather ominous large swells surging through the gap, it was necessary to judge carefully when to make a dash. After several false alarms, the four started paddling furiously into the breach between coral banks easily visible in the clear water. Then out of nowhere a huge wave formed behind the runabout. Laurie was at the stern and saw the wave looming over head, so he shouted, "Abandon ship" and promptly leapt into the sea.

The three remaining on board were swamped in foam and water and dashed to the floor. The folding chairs disappeared overboard as the runabout rode the swell and was swept on a wild uncontrolled dash over the reef and towards the beach. What a ride. The runabout surfed the swell just like a regular Australian surfboat. Inside the reef it was calm, and the team took stock of the gear that was luckily still on board. No one was hurt. But where was Laurie? He soon appeared swimming through the waves breaking on the outer edge of the reef. He made it up on top of the reef and stood in knee deep water and tried to wade across the uneven coral reef towards the shore but suddenly disappeared down a hole, reappeared and then was swamped by the next wave. Incredibly, after a series of ups and downs and disappearing down holes in the reef he made it inside to the calmer, shallow water. The others cheered every fall, plunge and lurch forward. A cut and bruised Laurie finally joined the now abandoned fishing party.

It was agreed that Bob and Pat should jog two km back around Moem Point to the camp, procure some fuel, and return in the little Red Renault. An hour later they duly reappeared and it was decided that Rick should take Laurie in the Renault to the Medical Centre to get his flesh wounds treated, while Pat and Bob would take the now refuelled and undamaged runabout back out through the reef, and scoot down the coast to the Sergeants Mess where the runabout was normally beached. Pat and Bob motored up and down looking out through the gap in the reef and finally gunned the motor and made a dash out into deep water.

This proved to be a poor decision and out of nowhere a huge wave loomed ahead. The runabout went up the face of the wave on about a seventy-degree angle and then flew freely through the air and crashed on to the water at the back of the wave. "No worries" said the Irishman from the back of the runabout. Bob had by this time lost all faith in the fishing skills of Pat and decided that the Irishman's boating skills were equally hopeless. Interestingly Pat's role at Moem was as a Driving Instructor.

A lesson had been learned – always check your fuel before setting off in a boat. The second lesson was not to use a flat-bottomed aluminium runabout as a surfboat in seriously big waves across a reef. So, the famed fished expedition returned with one bloodied body, three trembling Nashos and no fish.

It was a good thing that Rick was conscripted into the Army rather than the Navy. He did not mind surfing but put him in a boat and he would quickly be seasick. Once, at Vanimo, Laurie meticulously planned a lakatoi fishing trip for a group of five. Rick was violently ill from almost the moment of setting off until the return. Additional bait was not required, and several sizeable Mackerel were caught while Rick lay there, head hanging over the side. Even more apparent was the total lack of sympathy from Rick's supposed mates. The best comradeship they could offer, as a brief aside, were words to the effect of, "You'll be right mate".

The second occasion was more embarrassing and occurred 300 metres offshore from the Moem Sergeant's mess and just beyond the fringing reef. Using a small Army dinghy, Rick and Laurie had anchored in what seemed a prime spot to relax and reel in some small but tasty fish. If any fish were caught, they would be given away. The swell was small but there was a reasonable wave motion running along the flat-bottomed craft. Rick lasted fifteen minutes before throwing up. Unlike Vanimo, this expedition was close to shore and the solution more obvious. After diving overboard Rick swam ashore and was on dry land in a matter of minutes, leaving Laurie to fish on alone. Rick's unease and contest with the sea continued for another 20 years.

Fishing was normally not a pastime on the Nasho Six's leisure agenda, and very few in the Sergeant's Mess seemed to have an interest in fishing in the Admiralty Sea right next door. Max recalls one excursion when the Army work boat took a large party out to Muschu Island off the coast for a picnic on the beach, swimming, and a general family fun day. On another day, Max and Laurie went out in a flat-bottomed assault craft with the two Education Lieutenants trolling for three and half hours above a reef. They caught one fish. No more fishing expeditions were undertaken and the only contact with Mackerel and Trevally after that was what the Mess Caterers provided on the BBQ plate.

47. Rick with a lakatoi (double outriggers, north coast, West Sepik design); 1966.

48. On the deck of HMAS Anzac during a visit to Wewak 1967. From left: Bob, Max, John, unknown crew member, Peter.

CHAPTER NINETEEN

ARMY versus NAVY

There has always been a healthy rivalry on the sporting field between the various arms of the defence forces, the Army, Navy and Air. Moem Barracks was no exception. Rivalry occurred for us when a Navy vessel made a port of call at Wewak. The LSM landing craft HMAS Arundel White was a regular visitor on recruiting trips or resupply runs but it did not have a large enough crew to mount a cricket or football team, and the Air Force was restricted to a few pilots going in and out on short visits.

A much-anticipated opportunity was the arrival of HMAS Anzac, the Navy's training ship. Inter-service matches were often bloody affairs on the football field so there was a degree of relief when it was agreed that on HMAS Anzac's next visit there would be a cricket match played under the 20/20 rules which are common today. Cricket in Australia in those days had a reverence normally reserved for national heroes and nation-forging events. Test matches against England were keenly followed as epic encounters. Shield cricket, the interstate competition, and District cricket, the local version, were followed with equal enthusiasm.

Every Australian town in the 1960s, no matter how small, had a cricket pitch and team.

The Navy of course considered itself the "Senior Service" and there was a hundred years of tradition riding on the outcome even if the match was being played in a remote corner of TPNG. As Moem Barracks only had a decrepit concrete strip in the middle of a makeshift athletics field, it was decided to play the match at a proper pitch in town. With 300 sailors on board, it was expected the Navy would put up a strong team probably with some potential Shield or State A-Grade cricketers. Various names were whispered later that night at the formal dinner in the Sergeants Mess, kindly hosted for the visiting Navy team by the RSM. This meal was awesome having luckily coincided with the Mess's normal Thanksgiving nosh-up.

At this stage, the score was one-all as the Education Sergeants easily won the eating competition and the Navy the drinking. The next day was the match when heroes would be made! Pete and Bob, with some cricketing behind them back home, were selected as openers for the Army team. There were nine other heroes in the 2PIR team but for this story they take backstage.

The Army team comprised NCO's who had trained for a day in preparation. This involved all who were trying out for the team bowling two overs each, batting and showing off their skills behind the wickets. At the end of the training a meeting was held, and a captain, vice-captain and selector were chosen. Bob who had always coveted the position as captain of a cricket team going back to primary and secondary school days, and had never held this position, took the bull by the horns and hinted he could act as captain. Pete jumped up and said, "I nominate Bob". There was a general nod of agreement, so Bob then jumped up and said, "I nominate Pete as Vice-captain". Again, there was a general nod of approval. An infantry Captain, who was quite a neat player, was looking miffed that he had been overlooked for these prestigious positions, so Bob quite correctly jumped up again and said, "I nominate Captain James as Selector". All agreed.

Missionaries and colonial officials across the Pacific had introduced cricket as a manly sport for "natives" to play and thereby learn how to be decent fellows and develop sportsmanlike qualities. The Mission cricket team from Kwato in the Milne Bay province was a famous example of this approach and they whipped all and sundry who passed through the China Straits and called at Samarai Island at the turn of the century. Trobriand Islanders in the eastern part of New Guinea had famously adapted the game to local customs and conditions and played all-day games with hundreds on each team, still known today as "Trobriand Island Cricket". Samoans also have their own mass-involvement, noisy, singing, dancing version of inter-village matches called *kilikiti*.

The appointed day for the "Big Bash" arrived and both teams assembled at the local Wewak cricket ground. Bob addressed the Army team but was decidedly nervous never having captained a cricket team, or anything, before in his life. The Wewak pitch was a first-class strip and had a turf wicket with lush mown green grass in the outfield. The Navy arrived late adding to the tension. They had already bragged how their spin bowling would rip through whatever the Army could put up. They arrived in full cricket creams, pressed neatly, and wearing cricket boots. This made the Army team look decidedly shabby as they were dressed in a variety of white t-shirts, baggy army khaki pants and not-so-white canvas "Volley" runners.

Bob won the toss and Pete shaped up as opening batsman to face the Navy pace attack. The Navy's opening bowler was a medium-pacer, quite quick and threatening, but Pete was waiting. Pete had played a bit of cricket and turned out to be more than a handy batsman. He smashed the first delivery to the boundary and then successive balls, all for four, and at the end of the over the Army were none for 12.

Bob then faced their number two bowler at the other end. Bob snuck a few early runs then played a steady hand while Pete continued in swashbuckling style at the other end until losing his wicket for a terrific 48 runs. By then the Army was one down for 60 runs. Bob went next, caught on the boundary for 30 runs. The batting order then struggled along to a respectable six for 150 and finally all out for 180 runs in the twentieth over. The Navy had been excellent in the field taking fine catches all over the ground.

After lunch, the Navy padded up. The target was quite reachable. Bob opened the bowling, and his left-arm medium swingers caused the Navy batsman a bit of trouble. Then Pete came in from the other end. Pete was 188cm tall with a wiry physique and could generate real speed pelting down balls from high above. The Navy were one wicket down for three runs after the first two overs. A few lucky LBW calls probably would not have survived today's video replays but soon the Navy were in trouble. Pete was starring, taking two brilliant catches in slips while resting between his overs. When Pete and Bob had bowled their quota of six overs each, for a total of six wickets, a bowling change took place and the Navy started to make a few runs. However, they were not good enough and were soon all out for 100 runs, well short of the Army score.

Pete was declared by all to be "Man of the Match". Everyone then headed back to the Sergeant's Mess for a few lively speeches and a serious attack on the Mess's supply of cold beer. It was agreed that both teams had performed admirably and maintained their respective Service's reputation for sportsmanlike behaviour and fair play. The match was a topic of conversation in the Mess for at least a week and everyone agreed, both "Regs" and Nashos, that the Army's reputation had been brilliantly maintained.

Pete never played cricket again, and Bob never captained a cricket team again, or any team for that matter.

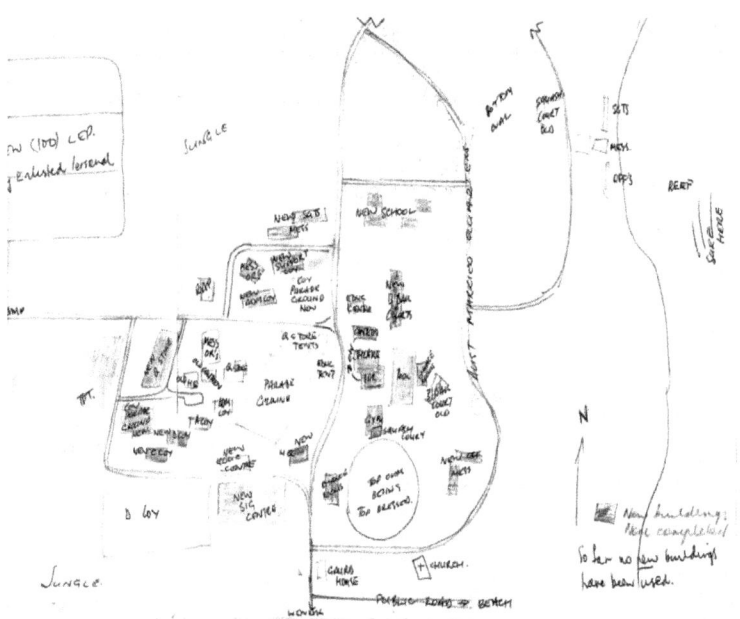

49. Moem Barracks showing new buildings to be opened at the year.
Source: A map sent home by Max to his parents, October 1967.

CHAPTER TWENTY-ONE

GOING HOME: AFTER NASHO

At regular reunions over the next fifty years, it was often claimed that National Service was not so bad after all and had some positive outcomes, and possibly was a success on the grounds of the contribution made to TPNG and specifically to 2PIR. National Service, with the period later shortened to eighteen months and then abolished in 1973, was a national policy that attracted criticism, but we are telling these stories now because there were also some beneficial consequences, limited perhaps, but visible here in the post-Nasho lives of the six from Wewak. Here is what happened to them after Nasho.

In November and December 1967, they flew back home for a period of leave and discharge and were no longer in uniform and no longer Sergeants. The six found there was no help or guidance given by the Army or by their respective Education Departments on how to settle back as civvies or pick up past civilian lives or re-start their teaching careers.

On his way home Bob had over-nighted at Taurama Barracks in Port Moresby, and then another overnight in Sydney before taking the final long flight to Perth. Margy was there and two months later they were married on the last day of December 1967. Early in 1968, having passed his Higher Certificate examinations, Bob returned to his old posting at Kukerin Primary school to teach the same grades, 3, 4 and 5, in the same classroom, same syllabus, same tests and reporting and the same small farming township. It seemed two years away doing Nasho had never happened. Bob and Margy moved into a house in town and started the work of building fences, gardens and a carport, and a family. Two daughters followed in 1969 and 1970. These were great years built around the seasonal cycle of community sports – tennis in summer, hockey for Margy and AFL for Bob in winter.

A fall in enrolments saw Bob leave Kukerin in 1973 and move to Mt Hampton, a one-teacher school in the remote east of the state. Mt Hampton consisted only of a school, crossroads, and a schoolteacher's house. Bob taught all seven-year levels. The nearest shops were 50km away. Water was carted in periodically by local farmers. With local donations Bob purchased a 240w generator and a 30m television mast and aerial and TV arrived in the bush. Most farms then did not have TV so educational programs, with Play School being the favourite, made going to school a hit. About 50 metres from the school was a bare patch optimistically called "the oval," so with Bob the driving force behind the P&C, a concrete cricket pitch was laid. Bob then took it further by organizing working bees to lay a pair of bitumen tennis courts beside the oval. This was a revelation as there had not been anything like this before to bring the community together. Lights were added much later and today both courts and oval are still in use. This was indeed a classic rural Australian community project, and typically shrugged off as just part of "country life".

Further changes took place in Bob and Margy's life with a third daughter being born. These were great years at Mt Hampton. Every Friday a local bus contractor would do a shopping run into Southern Cross, but he had a slight drinking problem when it came to driving back. So, Bob stepped in and solved the problem. There was no cash changing hands but after he drove the bus back to Mt Hampton, Bob would be taken to a nearby shearing shed where a tender fat lamb awaited. An hour of butchering later, and the Masons had two weeks supply of fresh meat. Margy was also busy being employed by the Education Department as Sewing Mistress, School Secretary, School Gardener and School Cleaner, the usual fate for teacher's wives in one-teacher rural schools. These tasks became a family chore with the three girls helping as well. This was like living on a farm, with weekends away visiting nearby towns to play football and tennis.

This lifestyle ended when Bob was promoted to Deputy Principal at Narrogin, a school with 400 pupils. This was like being Sgt Mason all over again. Bob taught a Class 7 in the mornings and then took on administrative roles in the afternoons, organized the sports program and coordinated visiting Graduate teachers. In 1975, Bob and Margy had their fourth daughter. Three years later Bob took another promotion and moved to Deputy Principal at Wagin District High School, responsible for the Primary section of the School. (Consolidated, District or combined Secondary and Primary schools were common across Australia in rural areas. Some continue today.) The family had to move 50km down the road to Wagin and Bob continued to teach in the mornings and do admin in the afternoons. Bob and Margy also bought an old house in Wagin and started the huge task of renovating, planning to stay put for ten years. But in 1981, Bob took another promotion, to Principal at Coolgardie Primary School, but not without long family discussions about the virtue of staying in Wagin where the four girls were happy with all their friends, compared to heading to Coolgardie which was rough around the edges and a typical mining town, regarded as the Wild West in WA at that time.

 Bob, now Principal Mason, rose to the challenge and the very nasty boys were warned, letters sent home to parents, and when all else failed the cane was applied. This was the old days of course, before corporal punishment was banned in schools. The boys did not like getting the cane and reformed almost overnight. After two years, Bob and Margy were looking for a change and their eldest daughter was suffering homesickness after being sent away at school in Perth. Memories of good times overseas in Papua New Guinea were revisited, and a year on teacher-exchange. Ontario, Canada, seemed like a good option to reunite the family and take a break from Coolgardie. 1983 was a great year. The temperature was minus 10 degrees when they arrived in Canada at a snow bound, forty-acre, one-hundred-year-old brick farmhouse just outside the small town of Credition. To the Masons it was a fairyland. Soon the girls were cross-country skiing and skating in ice-covered ponds. Wow!! Bob drove 20km to his school every day while the girls caught the big, yellow bus to Steven Central School 8km away. Margy stayed home, spending hours planning weekend adventures. The favourite trip was nearby to London, on the Thames River in Canada, but summer trips were further afield to Canada's eastern provinces. Bob found Canada to be a big country with warm-hearted folk and over the years several return visits took place, with Bob and Margy's youngest girl spending a year in Calgary in 2006.

In 1984, Bob finally headed to the big city, Perth, and took up a series of Principal positions at South Terrace, Booragoon, and Como, finally retiring in 2007. The four girls all completed their university studies and Margy trained as a medical receptionist, working at an Applecross clinic for twenty-five years. There is hardly a local family in nearby suburbs that Margy has not met along the way. In retirement, Bob and Margy are now busy with their ten grandsons. So, from humble beginnings in the Australian bush, an incredible journey with a large family and six Army mates has led from Mt Magnet, Kukerin, Wagin, Mt Hampton and Coolgardie, to Papua New Guinea and finally to Perth.

On his return Rick spent 1968 at the University of Western Australia on an Army scholarship, being paid the Basic Wage, and married Helen in August of that year. This marriage of over fifty years led to three children and seven grandchildren. In 1970, Rick returned to TPNG as a young married man with his wife and child, to work as a psychologist in various locations. Rick returned to Moem several times, being invited on one occasion to dinner by Sgt John Brown, teammate and the 2PIR AFL team's star full-forward. The Adjutant of the Regiment, who was also there at the dinner, at one point in the evening commented that the Army experience must have been good and helped young men like Rick to become 'more of a man'. The Major then struggled with Rick's reply that he had been fortunate in his posting and that the Army had not damaged him as it had others. Rick went on carefully to suggest that uniforms and stripes are not mandated on the journey to adulthood, and that other learnings were at least equally helpful, if not more so, to growing up. The conversation was well-received on all sides, although the topic soon changed back to past victories and great footy matches.

Rick's role in TPNG in 1970-72 was Regional Psychologist with the Public Service Board, responsible on the New Guinea mainland for recruitment, counselling, research, psychological testing, and in Lae for services at the Psychiatric Ward at Angau Memorial Hospital. Rick also had the good fortune to briefly supervise Kipling Uiari, TPNG's first Psychologist, who had just graduated in Queensland. Kipling took over Rick's role and went on to have an illustrious career before sadly dying suddenly on Port Moresby golf course at the age of 48.

In 1972, Rick was promoted to a new role as Clinical Guidance Officer with the TPNG Education Department. This role was largely ill-defined and covered the entire Territory – Papua, New Guinea, Highlands, and Islands. Rick travelled widely speaking at thirteen teacher training colleges scattered across TPNG, with Tari being a standout visit. He also visited Manus Island (now an Australian offshore detention Centre) several times. Another key role was acting as facilitator for programs to identify, rapidly train and promote teachers considered suitable for accelerated advancement to senior positions in the TPNG Education department. The localisation of Education was part of the preparation for Independence and unearthed a pool of incredibly talented Papua New Guineans. These experiences also made Rick aware that he was inadequately trained, too young, and to poorly equipped to continue as a Psychologist in TPNG. Rick terminated his contract in December 1972 and submitted a recommendation to the Director-General that he be replaced by three local officers, who could offer far more culturally aware service. At the time, local officers were paid three-eighths the salary of an Australian. This proposal was ignored in 1973, but something along these lines was put in place in 1974.

Relatively unscathed after Nasho at Moem, Rick openly admits that he was frequently out of his depth as a civilian Psychologist when he returned to TPNG as a civilian. On his return to WA, Rick continued to work as a School Psychologist, in metropolitan and rural settings for a number of years. In the rural position he was the sole school psychologist for 44 wheat-belt schools. Tired of being regarded as a 'visitor', and often faced by teachers and families seeking advice but with unrealistic expectations, Rick finally decided to return to classroom teaching. He became a Deputy Principal then a Principal. Nowadays Rick works part-time as a consultant to the Education Department, largely in Principal merit selection processes as well as doing some specialised voluntary counselling work in another area.

Rick admits he was not really interested in being a soldier and that usually he was able to switch off. He recalls meeting, in 1980, a Victorian Nasho friend, Noel Fitzgerald who had been posted to ASCO, the Army Services Canteens Organisation. Noel came with a friend to Perth to see Rick for the first time since they were recruits in the same cubicle at Puckapunyal. They met at Laurie's Bowman's house. Noel introduced Rick to his friend as "unflappable, the only guy I met who the Army did not touch". Rick is not sure if he agrees. Rick also wonders whether his propensity to ponder and over-analyse everything originated in his years in TPNG. Was it these years that made him concerned about issues such as political correctness; racist behaviour and views which are often held by people without understanding or experience; views that are firmly either black or white when complex topics suggest exploration of the grey; he worries about consumerism and an obsession with possessions, and the growing gap between the haves and the have-nots? Rick's attitude today is that he was fortunate to leave the Army unscathed, but that he certainly benefitted from the Wewak experiences and the close friendships with his Moem mates in things military, educational, sporting and more.

Historians and Political Scientists have argued that the granting of independence in PNG was too early but in Rick's view delaying independence may not have helped, merely delaying the troubles experienced by all new, artificially constructed nations emerging out of the colonial era. PNG, the land of Rick's second son's birth, is a special place on this earth. It is still in his heart. He is saddened by the PNG of today where tribal conflicts, the *wantok* factor and isolation issues have brought corruption, crime, and lack of progress to this new nation. Papua New Guineans showed amazing courage in supporting Australian soldiers in the dark days of WWII and among their progeny are people of great intelligence and integrity who, Rick argues, will one day make this earthly diamond a more secure and stable place, while simultaneously treasuring a very long history and amazing diversity.

In Victoria, Max also took a new direction but not of his own choice. His intention on returning was not to go back to the small one-teacher school in the Mitta Valley in north eastern Victoria where he had taught in 1965, but to head for Horsham, a large town in the Wimmera where his parents had recently moved and where he could play football with the local team, then coached by John Beckwith, a former Melbourne player and AFL star. This was not to be as Max was plucked from this planned rural odyssey and thanks to a far-sighted Victorian Director of Education, sent instead to Monash University to do a BA Honours degree. The Director was keen to make an example of Max, and to show

how the Education Department looked after its returning "heroes". So, for the next five years, Max studied History, taught part-time at a suburban Primary School during university vacations and played footy in the Mornington Peninsula League, winning a Premiership, a League B&F and several club B&F awards. In 1973, he graduated and his life took another turn when he was unexpectedly appointed Lecturer in Asian and Pacific Studies at the same campus from which he had graduated with a Trained Primary Teachers Certificate in 1964, now re-named the State College of Victoria at Frankston. Teaching and research in Pacific Island History became his career path for the next forty-five years. In 1988, Max moved to QUT in Brisbane where he thought of staying perhaps three years but ended up enjoying Queensland so much, he stayed for 22 years, including a year on exchange at UPNG in Port Moresby in 1992. In 2010, he headed to the University of the South Pacific, located in Suva, Fiji, and after a six-year contract decided to make Brisbane his retirement home.

His contacts with the Pacific had become stronger over the years, especially after a ten-year Japanese-funded professional development program for Pacific Island history teachers (with his mate Grant McCall from Sydney), a year teaching in Port Moresby, taking Australian students on an immersion fieldwork course each year at various villages around the Pacific, and writing articles, books, book chapters and reports. His PhD thesis was on photography during PNG's colonial history, an interest he still maintains by giving presentations at conferences, and as a Guest Speaker on cruise ships around the islands. He never married, ignoring the advice of his PIR mate, Sgt Peter Mamare, in a letter to Max in August 1968 to "get married boy and settle down".

50. Reunion, Manly beach, NSW, 1970; John, Sandra, Max, Peter, Bob, Lorellyn, Margy; Photo by Laurie Bowman.

51. Reunion 1998. The effigy was for Rick who was unable to attend. On the far right is Zoltan, the seventh Nasho Chalkie at Moem in 1966, who joined in for this reunion.

Max considers his life took a direction that could not have been imagined prior to his Nasho years, but had changed dramatically not by design, but by a set of fortuitous circumstances. The first being his birth date being drawn in the Nasho ballot. Then being chosen to go to join the Chalkiues in TPNG. Then in Melbourne in early 1968 at an Education Department de-briefing for returning Nashos, Max was the only ex-Nasho to put up his hand to say he had passed Matriculation. The Director of Education intervened and sent him to university, forestalling what would have been a country football career, country school headmastership, probably marriage and a rural family. Instead, he gained a BAHons, MA and PhD and enjoyed a career lecturing in Pacific Island History in Victoria, Queensland, PNG, and Fiji. Over the years he has returned several times to PNG for workshops, conferences, a friend's marriage and on cruises. He always felt at home.

Peter returned home to NSW and settled back into Newcastle and completed the first half of a degree at Newcastle University, thanks to a one-year Australian Government Commonwealth Scholarship in recognition of National Service. He completed the rest of the degree part-time after resuming secondary teaching in Newcastle for the next 32 years. Sport continued to play a major role in Peter's life – squash, golf, and surf lifesaving, serving for a long time as a SLSA instructor and examiner. At the same time, he enjoyed 15 years of triathlons (now known as the "Ironman" competition) and representing Australia in his age group at World Championships in Surfers Paradise and Perth. Pete recalls he was a triathlete first and a teacher second. As a good Newcastle boy, he also played rugby union and in 1968 played in a premiership with "The Waratahs", a local team (not for the NSW squad!)

Looking back over fifty years of sport, teaching, marriage and living in Newcastle, Peter now enjoys his retirement, with children, grandchildren, regular overseas vacations, touring around Australia, camping, trekking, and tackling walking tracks in New Zealand. Like his six Wewak mates, he enjoys keeping in regular contact, traversing the continent, and visiting for reunions, weddings, and births.

Laurie left Wewak a couple of weeks after Bob, Rick and Pete, flying to Moresby, then direct by jet to Sydney and on to Perth all in one day. It was a long flight but exciting to be home. Like Bob he was engaged and had made arrangements to be married. Laurie married Lorellyn on 29 Dec 1967. The wedding was attended by Rick and his future wife Helen and Bob and Marg who were to be married the next day. On the first day of their honeymoon Laurie came down with a severe bout of malaria which lasted several days, just to add a little reminder of PNG. They went on to have two children, Craig born in 1970 and Melissa in 1971. Laurie thinks one benefit of being in Nasho as a group 6 Sergeant was being on a pay scale which was way above what a WA teacher would earn and in Wewak there was nothing to spend it on. As a result, Laurie had saved a sizeable amount to start married life. After discharge Laurie returned to education as a Year 6 teacher in a large city primary school. There were about 200 children in Year 6, steamed according to academic level and Laurie ended up with Class 6D, with 51 children from the bottom 25% and mostly boys so the army discipline came in handy. One notable posting in the early 1970's was for three years to the remote Indigenous Australian community of La Grange with Laurie as Principal and Lorellyn teaching junior primary. Along for the ride were two children still of pre-school age. It was easy to draw parallels between that and teaching in 2PIR as English was a second language for most of the 100 children in the school. Indeed, one family was brought into the community from the Western Desert having lived as their ancestors did for thousands of years. These children were expected by the Education Department to just assimilate into the school.

Living at La Grange and at postings in the iron ore towns of the Pilbara and later in the wheat belt engendered a lifelong love of the outback and travel for Laurie and family. Laurie maintained close contact with his WA counterparts, Rick, and Bob, with occasional visits from the "easterners". (WA lingo for mates from NSW and Victoria) Being in New Guinea had some influence on Laurie's career in education as most of his postings were to remote rural places, returning to the city school postings only when their children started studies at university.

What good did "Nasho" do in the long run? – John responds to the question by arguing that the six Chalakies were not "brothers in arms" in the sense of being on the battlefront as real soldiers, but they did share unusual experiences in the Army in TPNG and have in many ways remained the best of friends, and indeed celebrated their fifty-year reunion in Perth in 2016. In practical terms, John notes he also came out of the Army with enough money to buy a new car. The bad news was that he came out of the Army with severe tinnitus, acquired on the rifle range in Wewak, when the Nasho Six fired pistols, rifles and machine guns with inadequate ear protection. The tinnitus and subsequent related bouts of depression continue to impact on John's life. On return, he stuck at secondary teaching for two years feeling poorly equipped to teach Year 12 Chemistry and Physics before moving into private enterprise, book retailing, the real estate market and later dealing in indigenous art. John married Sandra and they had three children. John agrees that Nasho turned his life upside down as a twenty-two-year-old. Unlike Bob, Pete, and Laurie, who stayed in primary and secondary teaching for their whole career, John thinks that Nasho was probably the motivation for other career choices he made on his return to Civvies.

Laurie answers the question, what did Nasho do for you, by saying that without the two years spent away he would have stayed in the cloistered atmosphere of schooling, spending his whole life from a five-year-old "prep" to his own career teaching. Laurie admits he was devastated when his marble was drawn in 1965, was very reluctant to go, and as many of his colleagues did, he expressed a strong dislike for all things military once he ended up in uniform. Laurie feels it was a sense of "Nashos versus Regs" that created the strong bond between the Wewak Six. Laurie also suggests that it was not until much later that they realised how fortunate they were to have ended up in such an adventure in TPNG and enjoy the enduring friendships which resulted. One memorable trip west by Pete and Max in 1971 resulted in travelling north with Bob and Laurie to Carnarvon Gorge and then east to remote Sandstone, Bob's childhood home and Danderaga sheep station with its amazing 16km square paddocks. For a while, contact between east and west was limited to the occasional letter, then in 1993 the bond came to the fore again when Laurie, on a caravanning trip, stayed with John in Kenthurst in Sydney. They managed to get Max down from Brisbane, Pete from Newcastle, and Bob to fly in from Perth for the first reunion in nearly two decades. Rick even made it in spirit as a cardboard effigy. The reunions have continued.

In retrospect, one of the strange aspects of serving for two years in an army camp with a thousand indigenous soldiers was the lack of close or enduring relationships between the six Nashos and local Papuans and New Guineans. Certainly at times there were friendships forged because of playing basketball or football, or working in the same infantry company environment, or games of darts in the Mess, but it must be admitted that the Nasho Six kept pretty much to their own company and age group for most of their stay in TPNG. Partly this was the result of Army protocols that delineated work roles and social mingling according to rank. 2PIR was in effect an Australian Army base although officially an arm of the emerging nation's security forces. This meant the racism existing in Australia between Indigenous Australians and non-Indigenous Australians and between immigrant communities and non-Indigenous Australians, despite claims that Australia was a harmonious multicultural society, also drifted over into the relationship between Australians and Indigenous soldiers in 2PIR. The Six Nashos are confident that they never displayed racist or discriminatory behaviour. They all recall being shocked to discover a "No dogs and no natives" sign outside the tavern in Wewak and being confronted with the racist attitudes of a Whites-Only club in Madang. But, throughout their time at Wewak, the Nasho Six did not develop many enduring friendships outside their own Australian group, a defensive reaction perhaps to the strictures and regulations which govern Army life generally. Max was probably the one who developed the most friendships outside Moem, as a result of his role in Army-Civilian sports development and because of shared interest with local Chinese and expats in basketball and surfboard riding, but even these friendships ended on returning to Australia.

At Moem Barracks the Nasho Six's behaviour was probably judged by other expatriates in and out of the camp milieu as typical of young, self-centered, "okker" Aussies, and while not overly close to indigenous soldiers, the Nasho Six did at times stretch the normal rules of engagement between Australians and Papua New Guineans in uniform.

All agree that the experience at Wewak did influence their later life choices and interpersonal relations with indigenous peoples. Rick returned to work in TPNG and developed a real love for the country and this perhaps influenced his working relationships with Indigenous Australians throughout his career. Max spent his whole career in the Pacific Islands, including periods researching and lecturing in Port Moresby and Suva in Fiji, and developing many life-long friendships with Islanders along the way, and Laurie went north in WA into the Kimberley as a teacher to work with Indigenous communities.

Had they made a contribution to TPNG? The elementary schooling provided in POE and PCOE classes and other lessons, possibly had a long-term impact on young 2PIR soldiers as they applied their new levels of western knowledge and communication as PNG approached independence and after. PNG certainly benefitted by having a better educated Army. Ted Diro's story reflects these changes. Lt Ted Diro was TPNG's first Indigenous Platoon Commander and served at Moem at the same time as the Nasho Six. His father had been a carrier on the Kokoda Trail. Lt Diro was a smart, ambitious, and dignified young officer and a rather quiet, thoughtful and well-respected soldier who rose through the ranks, going from Platoon to Company Commander at 2PIR and then becoming a Brigadier and Commander of the PNG Defence Forces later in his career. He then entered politics and became Deputy Prime Minister of the country. His journey included a Knighthood and being considered in 2017 for the position of Governor General. Sir Ted's career has been accompanied by some controversy, but this has been the norm during the troubled pathway since PNG's independence. There is a Ted Diro Primary School at Murray Barracks, now accommodating about 1600 students. Few can lay claim to such an exciting, successful, and challenging career pathway.

The Nasho Six certainly added to 2PIR's esprit de corps by starting up sports competitions and by maintaining open relationships across ranks and language groups. The lack of racism and refusal to abide by "Masta-boi" (European – Native) codes of behaviour set the Nasho Six apart from other Australians in the Territory and possibly that allowed Papua New Guineans to see there could be a different society and regime to that which had prevailed for the previous sixty years. This message had been starkly bought to attention after a visit by Army Minister Malcolm Fraser when he demanded that Australians serving in the PIR needed to interact more often and positively with Papua New Guineans, and a message came down through the RSM that if this was unacceptable to anyone in the Sergeant's Mess and they wanted to leave, they would be transferred immediately. No one took up the offer to leave, but there did not seem to be an improvement in Australian-PNG relationships as a result of the Fraser's warning.

The Nasho Chalkie scheme in TPNG was a well-intended concept taking advantage of a captive cohort of trained teachers and probably achieved its aim of rapidly bringing the PIR up to the standard soon to be required of a new nation and strategic ally of Australia. It made good use of professionally trained young men whose time and expertise would have otherwise been largely wasted had they stayed in khaki in Australia or fought in an ugly war in Asia. With hindsight it is reasonable to suggest that had Australia or the Army funded a further cohort of 300 teachers to stay in the PIR for the three years through to independence in 1975, then PNG would have been even better equipped with a large, educated pool ready to assist in the military and public service as localisation evolved.

Nasho or conscription was a significant factor in many young lives. With the Nasho Six now in their early seventies the most enduring legacy has been the friendship forged between mates, now sustained over more than 50 years. The Wewak Six have been there for each other in times good and bad; in sickness and in health. Rick considers that the friendship between the Nasho Six has been a privilege not diminished by banter, inevitable jibes, tall stories, and fading memories. The tales from the *sak-sak* in this book in Rick's view have the capacity to add more cement to a bond which began and developed under the umbrella of conscription.

The Sergeants Mess at Moem no doubt recovered quickly from the brash, noisy, confident, and sometimes uncouth behaviour of the first Nasho Education intake. By the time the hardcore "Regs" realised the original Nasho Six had gone, the next bunch of Nasho Chalkies had moved into the Mess, or into Married Quarters. Looking back the Wewak Six agree that doing Nasho in the late 1960s was a momentous two years, and that lives did change and were influenced in many good ways by the experience. Despite the almost universal dislike of conscription, and the strange manner in which reference to Nasho disappeared almost immediately from public language and discourse, some argue Australia should re-instate National Service. (For example, see; https://www.facebook.com/Bring-back-National-Service-Australia-565258743523889/. The Australian War Memorial website also has a short history of the Nasho scheme; https://www.awm.gov.au/articles/encyclopedia/viet_app).

The Wewak Six were twenty-year-olds when in some States and Territories of Australia their mates had only just begun to vote, drink and drive, and they were isolated overseas in a foreign country at the age of 20 to 22 when most young men were expected to marry and settle down and pursue the same career for their entire working life. The Nasho Six were torn from this comfortable, predictable routine and sent overseas to a place they had barely heard of before they arrived. Max is also certain that Nasho changed his life path from being a primary teacher, married and happily enjoying country life somewhere in Victoria, to having taught a number of amazing university graduates in two States - Victoria and Queensland – and three countries – in Australia, Papua New Guinea, and Fiji. John also switched paths away from teaching and became a businessman, art dealer, and investor. Laurie, Bob, Rick, and Pete all stayed in education and had equally rewarding post-Nasho lives in both urban and rural settings. A "what if" approach to history would ask how lives might have been different; for example, what might have happened 'if' the six had not been called-up, not sent overseas to Papua New Guinea, and even more so, not posted to a remote army base on New Guinea's northwest coast.

There is no answer to this conjecture, but all agree that being at Moem Barracks, Wewak in 1966 and 1967 affected them in some way, both positively and negatively, and still does.

52. L to R: Max, Pete, Rick, Bob, Laurie, and kneeling, John, at the TPNG Nasho Chalkies Reunion, Port Stephens, NSW, 2016.

CHAPTER TWENTY-TWO

FINAL COMMENT on DOING NASHO in NEW GUINEA

The policy of sending 300 Nasho teachers, or 'Chalkies' to Papua New Guinea certainly had an impact on the Pacific Islands Regiment, and on TPNG in the years leading up to independence, but there is an element of confusion over whether the two years "Nasho" had a subsequent impact on the post-Nasho life of the six young men in the stories related here.

The jolly tale of the six Nashos growing up and experiencing Army life in an overseas posting in TPNG is related here but in no way diminishes the service and contributions, intent, service, and valour of other Nashos. This tale of six young men sent far away and then dumped back in the system, is a success story from that era, but perhaps that is a judgment the reader should make after considering what happened in Papua New Guinea as it continues to make the transition from colonial territory to independent nation, and what happened to the Wewak Six when they came back to Civvy Street.

Bob thinks that he was amazingly lucky that his birthday was drawn out in the Nasho birthday lottery and like the rest of the

Wewak Six he considers both Nasho and the fifty years of mateship afterwards to be a success story. Bob is sure the two years of army discipline and camp life helped him through tough school situations in his teaching career. Peter Suna considers that he also is one of the "lucky ones". Life in the Armed Forces was a positive experience and as a young provincial city boy, it gave Peter the stability of a home, Sergeant's Group 6 pay and a solid financial base for the future. But above all, Peter notes that Nasho gave him five great mates: "Fingers", "Pants", "Sheets", "Larry" and Max!

Peter's opinion is that he can think of no better group to share the journey of life with, as these ex-Nasho blokes were there for those two years in TPNG, but also for each other since then for all of life's ups and downs. Despite the geographical distances between them since discharge in 1967, the bond of mate-ship forged in their Nasho Wewak years remains in place still more than fifty years later.

Initially the impact on six young men of being in New Guinea for most of their Nasho service was dramatic. Moem barracks was not only remote within TPNG but 2PIR was a newly formed battalion in a new barracks in an Australian colony just nine years away from independence. The educational opportunities opened by the Army's Education Program in basic English and Social Studies, benefitted the soldiers and some went on to higher ranks in the Army, into national politics and private enterprise. The long-term impact of improved education opportunities as TPNG moved rapidly towards self-government and then on to full nation status was therefore significant. The Army planner who thought up the idea of sending trained teachers caught up in Nasho to TPNG to expand education for the Pacific Islands Regiment was identified by Darryl Dymock in his book on the "Chalkies", as Brigadier Ian Hunter, the head of TPNG Command, an innovator who should have been given a medal. What a stroke of genius.

Towards the end of 1967, the Nasho Six at Moem had returned to Australia. Neither the Army nor the respective State Education Departments had a strategy in place to facilitate this transition, typified by the proforma letter sent out by the Directorate of Army Education in Canberra as the posting of the inaugural cohort of Nasho Chalkies to TPNG came to an end (See Appendix A).

Confusion continued with Bob's discharge certificates unable to decide if he was a Sergeant or a Temporary Sergeant (See Appendix B and C) and Max's discharge certificate incorrectly listed the number of days served in New Guinea. It took a long time for National Service to be acknowledged in Australia and it was not until 2001, that an Anniversary of National Service 1951-1972 Medal was finally struck to acknowledge the 187 National Servicemen who died in active service, the 1,500 wounded and the 300,000 who had been conscripted. It has been awarded to 127,000 Australians. The letter Bob received from the then Minister of Veterans Affairs, stated the medal honoured his "service to the nation". (See Appendix D)

In early 1968, after a brief letter from their respective Education Departments indicating a city or rural posting for the coming year, they were expected to just fit straight back into their pre-Nasho lives. They did, but their lives also took on unexpected and rewarding diversions, and that perhaps is the real benefit of living in another country, and of a military conscription program.

APPENDICES

A   Certificate of Discharge for Bob Mason, Feb 1968
B   Interim Certificate of Discharge for Bob Mason, Feb 1968
C   Letter from Army Directorate of Education, Sept 1967
D   Letter from Minister of Veterans Affairs, nd.
E   Why is Australia involved in Vietnam? AACE Current Affairs hand-out 1968
F   Moem Area Sports Notices, 25 Sept 1967, 2PIR Moem Barracks (edited by Max)

A   CERTIFICATE OF DISCHARGE FOR BOB MASON, FEB 1968

RAR -~~RAREACMP~~

AAF - A.199
Revised Sep, 1966

AUSTRALIAN MILITARY FORCES

INTERIM DISCHARGE CERTIFICATE

W-1/66-137

This is to Certify

that the discharge from the Permanent Military Forces of

Army No 5714151   Rank T/SGT   Initials R.J.   Surname MASON
(BLOCK CAPITALS)

has been duly authorized

Authority: 194/67   Command WESTERN   Dated 9-11-67

Reason: EXPIRATION OF SERVICE IN RAS (NS) NSA 27 (2)

and I hereby certify that the discharge was effected on 1-2-68

_____ CAPT.   OC WCPD.   _____
Signature and Rank of Officer   Appointment   Date

Specimen Signature of Soldier _Mason_

This certificate is of a temporary nature and indicates only that the above-named has served in the Permanent Military Forces. A Discharge Certificate will be forwarded to the following address:

P.O.
KUKERIN.

710475—200 Pads of 50 in Trip

B INTERIM CERTIFICATE OF DISCHARGE FOR BOB MASON, FEB 1968

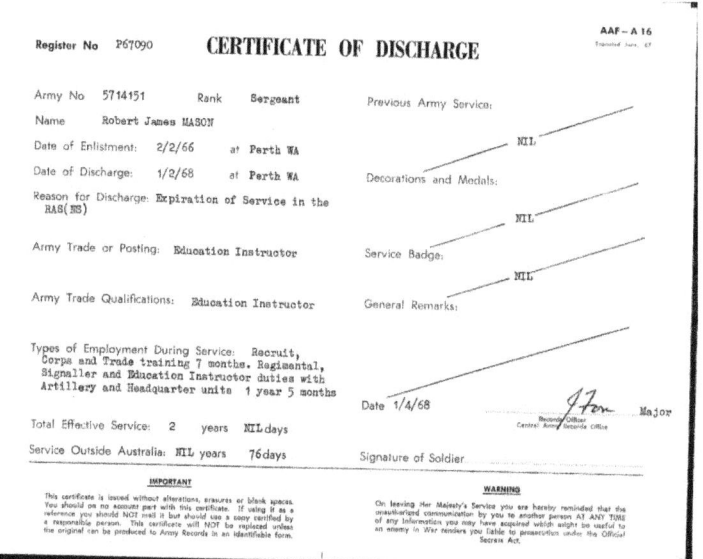

C   LETTER FROM ARMY DIRECTORATE OF EDUCATION, SEPT 1967

From: Brig E.C. GOULD, O.B.E., Director of Army Education.

AUSTRALIAN MILITARY FORCES

Telephone:
65-2966

MILITARY BOARD
(Adjutant-General)

Quote in reply:
D/O

Directorate of Army Education,
Army Headquarters,
Russell Offices,
CANBERRA, A.C.T.

1st September, 1967.

Sgt R.J. MASON,
PNG Command.

Dear Mr. Mason,

Your period of service with the RAAEC is drawing to a close and I feel it is time I wrote to you and to your fellow NCO's in PNG Comd to tell you how much I appreciate the generous spirit which you have manifested in carrying out the most important task which you were given.

Not only have you shown excellent spirit but you have also carried out your duties with exemplary efficiency.

You have made a notable contribution to the advancement of the Pacific Island soldier and I hope and trust that in return you have made a personal and professional gain from your contact with him.

The ARA members of the Corps join with me in thanking you for your assistance and in wishing you continued success in your career.

I do hope you will keep in touch with us through the RAAEC Association which it is my intention to form in the near future. You will, I trust, excuse this letter being a stereotyped one. My sincere thanks go to you individually. I regret I have not the time to make each letter an individual one.

Yours sincerely,

E. C. Gould

D LETTER FROM MINISTER OF VETERANS AFFAIRS, ND

MINISTER FOR VETERANS' AFFAIRS
MINISTER ASSISTING THE MINISTER FOR DEFENCE

PARLIAMENT HOUSE
CANBERRA ACT 2600

Mr RJ Mason
2b Sixth Avenue
APPLECROSS WA 6153

Dear Mr Mason,

On behalf of the Federal Government, I would like to congratulate you on the award of your *Anniversary of National Service 1951-1972 Medal*. It is both a physical reminder of your service to the Nation and an enduring remembrance of the heartfelt appreciation of the Government and your fellow Australians for that valuable service.

The *Anniversary of National Service 1951-1972 Medal* commemorates the 50th anniversary of the introduction of post-World War II national service. Today, the two periods of post-World War II national service are remembered as significant and valued events in Australia's history and development as a nation. Indeed, during the twenty-one year period that covered the two schemes, 187 national servicemen made the ultimate sacrifice for their country, while approximately 1500 were wounded during their service.

I would also like to use this opportunity to encourage you to contact your local Federal Member or Senator to arrange for the formal presentation of your medal. Presentation of your medal by a representative of Government will provide an appropriate occasion for your family, friends, and local community to express their gratitude for the service rendered by national servicemen.

You may find it useful, if you have the facility, to visit the Australian Electoral Commission (http://www.aec.gov.au) or Australian Parliament House (http://www.aph.gov.au) internet sites for contact details of your local Federal Member or Senator. Alternatively, you may find the information in your local White Pages Directory.

Yours sincerely

Danna Vale

DANNA VALE MP

E WHY IS AUSTRALIA INVOLVED IN VIETNAM? AACE CURRENT AFFAIRS HAND-OUT 1968

AACE 1 CURRENT AFFAIRS

WHY IS AUSTRALIA INVOLVED IN VIETNAM?

REASON The most important fact in this matter is that we are there by invitation, a specific request by the Govt of SVN to the Govt of Australia.

AIM Our aim is to help the SVN people fight and repel aggressors so that they, the people of SVN will be given the chance to choose the form of govt they desire.

P.M. REASONS The PM said in a speech to Parliament a 5 point plan to answer the answer the above questions, they cover the reasons.
1. Our first aim is to free SVN of the aggressors.
2. To free the people from being forced to live under an imposed system of government.
3. To make clear to all our allies that the Aust govt will stand by its allies if it is asked to do so.
4. To deny the spread of Communism in SE Asia and at the same time help to encourage those moderate and those democratic countries of SE Asia who might tend to be intimidated by the Communists.
5. Firstly we seek a peaceful settlement in SVN not a widening of the war, or war against NVN.

Other Points
1) A successful resistance and victory over aggression in SVN will help the keeping of security and the safeguarding of peace throughout SE Asia.
2) We have a responsibility to our allies - mainly the US (who we support in policy and are joined with by treaties)
3) The region where this conflict is; strategically, as well as economically and geographically important to Australia. Thus it might be said that it is in our own interests, as well as that of SVN that the the peace is maintained and the spread of Communism halted.
4) Chinas foreign policy is that it must surround itself with pro - comm countries to help its own internal security- this means perhaps more conflicts like SVN. A defeat here will provide a deterrant to any possible spread of comm and loss freedom of other SE Asian countries.
5) What would be the consequences if we were not to participate? This is in itself an imp reason.
   i) We would lose face in eyes of our allies in SE Asia and elsewhere.
   ii) There would be a loss of freedom of millions of people.
   iii) A spread of communism.
   iv) A loss of confidence among SE Asian countries.

SUMMARY We are here because we were invited, but why must we accept?
1. It will give freedom to the SVN people.
2. It will stop the spread of communism- and ensure the security of other and freedom of other SE Asian countries.
3. We must honour our alliances.
4. It is in our own interests,

F MOEM AREA SPORTS NOTICES, 25 SEPT 1967, 2PIR MOEM BARRACKS (EDITED BY MAX)

BORAM 657

R211-1-2

Distribution List

A2

Second Battalion
The Pacific Islands Regiment
Moem Barracks
WEWAK   TPNG

25 SEP 67

MOEM AREA SPORTS NOTICES

RESULTS WEEK 18 SEP to 24 SEP

1. a. Basketball

   (1) Womens Grand Final
   U.S.C. 21 d MOEM 1 9

   (11) Mens Grand Final.
   EDUCATION 31 d PIMQ BOTTOM 29

   b. Inter Company Sport Wednesday 20 SEP
   (1) Basketball
   B COY 44 d Admin COY 26
   Admin COY 11 35 d Sp COY 29
   B COY 50 d BnHQ 28

   (11) Softball
   Edn 14 d Admin COY 11

   (111) Soccer
   A COY v Admin COY (game was cancelled)

   (1V) Volleyball
   Admin COY 2 d A COY 0

   c. Weekend Sport

   (1) Basketball

   PIR 1 d CYO (on a forfeit)
   PIR 11 64 d Schoolies 38

INDEX

16mm, 17, 144, 157, 158, 159
16mm film, 144
2PIR, 6, 9, 11, 14, 58, 62, 77, 81, 84, 87, 101, 102, 103, 104, 107, 108, 111, 113, 127, 128, 137, 159, 164, 165, 167, 168, 169, 177, 180, 190, 200, 210, 215, 219, 227, 229, 230, 231, 236, 239, 251
500, 17, 77, 159, 237
Adelaide, 13, 27, 55, 56, 57, 59, 60, 61, 62, 147
AFL, 5, 26, 40, 73, 77, 156, 161, 162, 165, 166, 168, 169, 171, 172, 177, 179, 181, 216, 219, 222
aircraft, 6, 9, 32, 54, 55, 88, 124, 150, 183, 184, 185, 188
Amanab, 16, 83, 115, 124
Ansett-MAL, 5, 142, 169, 187
anti-tank, 140
Armoured Corps, 62
Artillery, 40, 43, 51, 53, 56, 81, 87
athletics, 163, 210
Aussie rules, 61
Bandiana, 9, 60, 109

basic training, 12, 21, 38, 40, 41, 43, 49, 50, 51, 53, 107, 109
basketball, 19, 27, 35, 47, 74, 77, 84, 87, 132, 161, 163, 164, 165, 166, 168, 171, 173, 179, 180, 229
battle-ready, 23, 92, 95, 111
bilum, 112, 121
Bingo, 17, 159
Bismarck Sea, 16, 69, 198
blisters, 119, 201
Bob Wriggley, 73, 83, 145, 156, 159, 168, 172
body surfing, 70, 160
Boeing, 63, 187
Bofor, 9, 55, 57, 59
Bomana WWII Memorial Cemetery, 65
Boram, 70, 84, 165, 175, 181
Bougainville, 74, 98
Brandi Beach, 16, 111
Brandi High School, 86, 167, 179
Brigadier Ian Hunter, 237
Browning, 108, 128
Buka, 73, 129, 166, 169
C&W, 16
cadets, 26, 28, 34, 43, 69
Canada, 218
Canberra, 22, 110, 237
Cape Wom, 74, 105

Caribou, 16, 81, 83, 92, 104, 110, 115, 118, 124, 137, 138, 142, 150, 187
Castellani's Paint, 200
CB, 5, 131, 132, 133, 134, 145
Cessna, 16, 92, 183, 185, 187
Chalkies, 9, 10, 11, 13, 23, 31, 62, 65, 73, 81, 92, 95, 101, 111, 114, 129, 139, 166, 173, 194, 201, 232, 234, 235, 237
Chimbu, 96, 106
CO, 5, 59, 64, 83, 89, 93, 97, 111, 134, 143, 145, 147, 160, 165, 167, 171, 183, 185, 186
Commanding Officer, 5, 101, 105
conscription, 7, 11, 15, 21, 36, 46, 232, 237
cordillera, 67, 113, 142, 184
cricket, 5, 17, 27, 79, 87, 161, 171, 184, 209, 210, 211, 212, 213, 216
crutch rot, 81
Current Affairs, 97, 111, 239
Darryl Dymock, 10, 237
darts, 10, 17, 73, 89, 105, 161, 196, 229
Daryl Howells, 105, 109, 197
DC-3, 5, 34, 67, 129, 142, 187
demonstrations, 7, 14

Didiman, 5, 12, 117, 180
dining-in nights, 151, 161
disease, 199
Dr Zhivago, 60
drone, 57
Dumbleyung, 19, 79
Duty Sergeant, 18, 106, 131, 132, 133, 134, 135, 144, 153, 155, 197
Education Centre, 9, 88, 92, 93, 95, 99, 100, 111, 133, 201
Education Corps, 9, 10, 43, 51, 59, 60, 63, 66, 67, 89, 96, 101, 117, 143, 194
Education Program, 236
English, 5, 6, 13, 17, 23, 34, 63, 92, 93, 94, 95, 96, 97, 98, 99, 101, 120, 154, 194, 227, 236
Enoggera, 60
Ferok, 16, 70, 160, 176
film projector, 144
fishing, 141, 195, 203, 205, 206, 207
Fokker, 187
fungal, 199
Goldie River, 9, 65, 74, 94, 103
Green River, 16, 92, 115, 124
grenade, 43
haus boi, 201
haus win, 9, 17, 75, 80, 81, 89, 97, 105, 132, 141, 157, 158, 159, 203
hepatitis, 137, 143, 147, 149, 201

Hercules, 140, 147, 150, 187
History, 39, 223, 225, 233
HMAS Anzac, 14, 150, 208, 209
HMAS Arundel White, 209
HMAS Sydney, 11
Holdsworthy, 9
Hollandia, 14, 104
Honda, 83, 84, 156
hospital, 34, 42, 69, 84, 87, 106, 143, 165, 177, 201
IACE, 5, 94, 98
Imonda, 124, 126
Indonesia, 13, 22, 56, 103, 104, 105, 110, 121, 122, 123, 127
infantry, 43, 44, 55, 56, 91, 92, 97, 137, 150, 163, 179, 211, 229
Irian Jaya, 12, 104, 117, 121, 137
jungle, 16, 42, 57, 67, 83, 88, 93, 108, 115, 119, 121, 123, 125, 126, 130, 186
Kapooka, 9, 32, 41
Keith Payne, 140
Kodak, 87
Korea, 104
Kukerin, 19, 27, 28, 79, 216, 219
Leitre, 119, 120
letters, 4, 11, 56, 81, 83, 97, 154, 180, 191, 218
Light Anti-Aircraft, 40, 55
lost at sea, 11
LPs, 89, 143, 191

LSM, 5, 136, 150, 209
M60, 42, 108
Madang, 117, 169, 170, 177, 179, 229
malaria, 84, 88, 169, 201, 226
Malaya, 22, 104
Malcolm Fraser, 14, 231
Mandated, 5, 22
Manly, 53, 54, 87, 224
Maprik, 127, 178, 194
medals, 11, 90
Medical Corps, 48, 49, 61, 62
Melbourne, 12, 13, 40, 41, 49, 55, 56, 59, 61, 62, 193, 222, 225
Minister of Veterans Affairs, 237, 239
Missionary, 31, 127, 149, 150
Missions, 94, 149
Moem Barracks, 9, 10, 12, 14, 18, 19, 30, 31, 32, 61, 65, 66, 67, 68, 78, 86, 87, 91, 93, 96, 97, 101, 105, 110, 111, 113, 140, 145, 159, 163, 165, 171, 173, 177, 179, 190, 199, 203, 209, 210, 214, 230, 233, 239
monsoon, 69, 70, 185
moped, 84
Moratorium, 7
movie nights, 148, 157, 179
Mt Hagen, 96, 103, 128, 129, 171, 179

Murray Barracks, 62, 65, 231
National Service, 7, 9, 11, 12, 14, 21, 28, 34, 40, 57, 215, 225, 233, 237
National Service 1951-1972 Medal, 237
Navy, 5, 11, 54, 150, 161, 206, 209, 210, 211, 212
New Guinea, 1, 3, 4, 6, 7, 9, 11, 13, 15, 19, 22, 29, 31, 40, 49, 59, 62, 64, 67, 88, 98, 103, 104, 105, 117, 124, 129, 130, 138, 142, 171, 179, 184, 186, 187, 190, 211, 220, 227, 233, 236, 237, *See* Papua New Guinea
Newcastle, 12, 28, 79, 225, 228
newspapers, 169, 190
nicknames, 168
North Head, 9, 40, 53, 55, 56, 57, 66
nurses, 69, 85, 141, 164, 177
Officer Training recruit, 50
Officers, 50, 62, 64, 67, 68, 69, 75, 85, 91, 99, 101, 105, 117, 138, 139, 142, 144, 152, 157, 160, 163, 183, 200
Officers Mess, 67, 85
one-teacher school, 25, 216, 222
Orderly Sergeant, 109, 131, 137, 179
Ordinance Corps, 48, 194

ORs Mess, 85
Ossima, 120
Owen Machine Gun, 42, 128
P&O, 87, 181, 188
Pacific Islands Regiment, 6, 9, 10, 22, 57, 62, 103, 235, 236
Pagei, 16, 104, 117, 118, 120, 122, 124
paludrine, 84, 85
Papua New Guinea, 6, 7, 12, 15, 22, 31, 59, 117, 158, 181, 187, 189, 190, 218, 219, 233, 235
patrolling, 56, 95, 113, 117, 130, 131, 134, 137, 142
patrols, 70, 74, 104, 113, 114, 119, 120, 122, 138, 142
PCOE, 6, 13, 92, 94, 98, 143, 145, 230
Peter Mamare, 73, 75, 84, 169, 223
photography, 87, 98, 112, 223
Pilatus Porter, 126
PIR, 6, 14, 15, 20, 22, 30, 63, 65, 81, 87, 90, 92, 94, 98, 101, 103, 110, 113, 128, 147, 159, 164, 167, 171, 223, 231
pistol, 108, 109, 128
POE, 13, 230
Police Motu, 23
Port Moresby, 9, 10, 11, 12, 13, 23, 60, 62, 63, 65, 66, 67, 81, 91, 94, 101, 103,

110, 111, 144, 157, 158,
  170, 171, 173, 189, 190,
  194, 215, 220, 223, 230
projector, 157
Psychology, 35, 48
Puckapunyal, 9, 13, 28, 34,
  37, 40, 41, 48, 49, 50,
  221
Queensland, 56, 158, 167,
  220, 223, 225, 233
racism, 75, 229, 231
radio, 16, 86, 140, 159,
  189, 190, 191
Readers Digest, 18
recruit training, 12, 22, 32,
  34, 38, 46, 49, 50, 65,
  108
Regs, 12, 13, 60, 72, 73,
  168, 196, 213, 228, 232
Renault, 61, 84, 176, 177,
  181, 192, 193, 194, 195,
  196, 197, 198, 205
rifle range, 27, 30, 43, 108,
  110, 227
ringworms, 202
rioting, 111
route march, 45
RSM, 5, 6, 62, 64, 74, 85,
  105, 106, 107, 108, 109,
  110, 111, 133, 134, 151,
  152, 153, 159, 197, 201,
  210, 231
rugby, 66, 87, 161, 166,
  173, 225
SACE, 6, 94, 99
sak-sak, 9, 16, 67, 69, 75,
  76, 92, 96, 134, 143, 147,
  151, 179, 199, 201, 232

SANFL, 57
Scotland, 33
search for plane, 191
Sepik, 9, 14, 31, 67, 77,
  113, 117, 138, 176, 181,
  185, 186, 189, 191, 208
Sergeants Mess, 9, 17, 61,
  66, 68, 72, 73, 99, 104,
  105, 110, 133, 140, 142,
  144, 151, 154, 155, 159,
  160, 164, 175, 179, 197,
  200, 205, 210, 232
shopping, 56, 154, 181, 217
Singleton, 9, 41, 50
SLR, 42, 43, 107, 108, 141
Smorgasbord, 154
Social Studies, 13, 92, 93,
  236
squash, 19, 35, 163, 164,
  165, 171, 173, 179, 225
St Kilda, 59, 159, 168
State Education
  Departments, 102, 237
STOL, 6, 186
study, 22, 27, 34, 77, 193
Sukarnopura, 14
surfing, 10, 40, 70, 79, 155,
  171, 176, 206
Sydney, 12, 29, 31, 40, 53,
  56, 57, 61, 66, 77, 87,
  215, 223, 226, 228
tanks, 9, 14, 44, 50, 85,
  180, 204
Taurama, 9, 63, 65, 66, 215
Teacher training, 27
Teacher Training
  Scholarship, 29

Teachers College, 27, 29, 31, 39, 49, 50, 51
Ted Diro, 230
Telefomin, 16, 112, 116, 142, 149, 182, 183, 185, 186
tennis, 19, 24, 27, 28, 39, 40, 164, 165, 180, 216, 217
tinea, 200, 201
Tinnitus, 109, 201, 227
tok pisin, 5, 6, 17, 96, 120, 127, 128, 189, 190
tombola, 138, 175
Torricelli Range, 178
triathlons, 166, 225
tsunami, 120
United Nations, 6, 14, 22, 103, 123
upela strait em gras, 96
Vanimo, 12, 18, 31, 62, 70, 72, 79, 81, 83, 91, 92, 94, 96, 103, 104, 113, 118, 119, 120, 122, 124, 179, 183, 185, 186, 187, 190, 197, 201, 206
VFL, 158, 171
Victor Harbour, 52, 57, 59
Victoria, 28, 39, 40, 41, 56, 60, 158, 160, 166, 180, 194, 222, 225, 227, 233

Vietnam, 7, 13, 14, 21, 22, 28, 37, 43, 44, 45, 49, 51, 55, 56, 57, 83, 97, 104, 105, 108, 111, 115, 140, 144, 239
volunteering, 183
WAFL, 36
Wantok, 6
Warrant Officer, 6, 64, 73, 84, 152 *see* WO
water-skiing, 83, 147
Watsonia, 9, 62
weather reporting, 142
West New Guinea, 12, 22, 92, 110, 117
Western Australia, 12, 23, 219
Wewak airport, 14, 87, 106, 180
Wewak Club, 175, 181
Wewak Hotel, 176
WO, 6, 73, 155, 167
Woodside, 9, 13, 40, 54, 55, 56, 59, 60, 63, 66
WWII, 5, 11, 22, 29, 32, 55, 65, 67, 85, 87, 103, 113, 128, 130, 162, 178, 222

www.ingramcontent.com/pod-product-compliance
Lightning Source LLC
Chambersburg PA
CBHW051422290426
44109CB00016B/1400